Teaching Introductory Programming

(with *Oh! Pascal!*)

Teaching Introductory Programming

(with *Oh! Pascal!*)

by Doug Cooper

UNIVERSITY OF CALIFORNIA, BERKELEY

W • W • NORTON & COMPANY
New York and London

ISBN 0-393-95447-1

W. W. Norton & Company, Inc.,
500 Fifth Avenue, New York, N.Y. 10110

W. W. Norton & Company Ltd.,
37 Great Russell Street, London WC1B 3NU

2   3   4   5   6   7   8   9   0

Table of Contents

Introduction

Welcome to the long-awaited accompaniment to *Oh! Pascal!* I've followed three guides in deciding what to include in this manual. First, what would I have liked to be able to lift from a teacher's manual when I began teaching? Second, what do colleagues usually ask me when I visit away from Berkeley? Third and finally, what aspects of teaching programming are usually neglected in print?

The material I would have liked to copy, and have included here, are short exercises suitable for quizzes (I've supplied nearly 600), and samples of working homework and exams. The questions I'm asked, and try to answer in a series of brief discussions, usually run along the lines of 'How can you successfully run a large course with neither staff nor equipment?' I think the main neglected aspect of teaching programming involves staff management, so I've included a series of discussions and handouts that are suitable for weekly staff meetings. An additional appendix contains comprehensible *vi* documentation.

In outline, the contents of this manual are:

- Chapter Highlights: a chapter-by-chapter outline of the text.
- Chapter Quiz: a collection of quiz/review questions for each chapter.
- Staff Meetings: some suggestions for weekly staff meetings, with handouts.
- Some General Advice: short discussions on a few topics of interest to the instructor.
- Appendix A: Facts *Every* Teenager Should Know About *Vi*; a tutorial introduction to the *vi* editor.
- Appendix B: My Course Exams; a sample first, second, and final exam from my freshman course.
- Appendix C: My Course Homework; weekly (almost) assignments and handouts from my course.

Where it refers to *Oh! Pascal!*, this manual describes the basic text. However, *Oh! Pascal!* contains a great deal of optional material that is suitable for a major's-level course in college, or has been recommended by the ETS Advanced Placement Examination for high-school courses. Such topics are best chosen selectively, depending on the pace of your course and your students' enthusiasm.

When in doubt, I have drawn from my own course. It is the all-purpose introduction to programming; notoriously difficult for the credit granted, required for a variety of majors, and permitted by the University to fulfill the 'quantitative reasoning' requirement. Its curriculum is fairly stable—programming in Pascal through arrays, with individual programs on the order of 500 lines, and group projects over 1,000 lines. My focus is on problem-solving, and on learning to evaluate a problem's amenability to computer solution. A growing trend is an emphasis on software engineering; my students are not liable to write programs after graduation, but they are likely to manage programmers, specify and evaluate software, and introduce computer applications.

This manual is being produced in a way that will make improvements to future printings quite easy. I invite comments and suggestions. I would also welcome additional material for a future edition of this manual, particularly if it is sent to me electronically.

Grateful thanks must go to the staff members, undergraduate and graduate, who have made my course work over the years. Doug Kidder and Charles Spirakis assisted with the preparation of this manual, while many other reader leaders and head TA's—Tim Learmont, Brian Bershad, David Bianco, Ramon Caceres, Herve DaCosta, and others—have contributed to the success of the course described herein.

Doug Cooper
Berkeley, July 1985

Computer Science Division, Evans Hall
University of California,
Berkeley, Ca. 94720
(dbcooper@BERKELEY, ucbvax\!dbcooper)

Teaching Introductory Programming

(with *Oh! Pascal!*)

General Tips

Here are some general hints that the first-time instructor may find useful. In my experience, it's the wide range of student ability in a large class (rather than a high or low class average), that makes teaching introductory students difficult. Most of my suggestions are intended to help smooth the curve, and to keep weaker students from falling behind.

Try to teach the book in chapter order.

Although some of the arrangement of material in *Oh! Pascal!* may be unusual, please give it a try. For instance, I don't introduce subprograms early because students are expected to write complex programs early; rather, I find that it's effective to have them learn some hard concepts (that soon *will* be essential) in the simplest possible setting. Similarly, the delayed introduction to *boolean* values and statements would be extraordinary in a FORTRAN-like course, but I think you'll find it works well when teaching Pascal to non-mathematical students. In any case, jumping around in the text is hard on the students, because it encourages them to accept not understanding sample programs. Naturally, this suggestion does not apply to any of the optional sections, which should be assigned at the instructor's preference.

Treat introductions to the text editor and system features as regular class work.

To many instructors, details of text editing or system operation are rightly seen as specialized technical material, distinct from the general academic content of a programming course. As a result, it's tempting to require that they be learned in 'do-it-yourself' assignments, no more worthy of class time than typing lessons would be. Unfortunately, some students tend to regard non-class material as non-essential material. True, these students are only cheating themselves; however, it translates into increased staff burden later in the term. Students who aren't comfortable with the basic tools of programming are not going to be the adventurous, enthusiastic students who are a pleasure to teach.

Use the blackboard carefully.

Not all students are real-time note takers. As a basic rule, try to have the board make sense at the end of the lecture. Some helpful techniques are: Start on the left-hand board and work toward the right. If you have a single, large board, draw heavy double lines to separate sections. If you use a blank section of a previously used board for a short example, draw a heavy double or triple line to separate it from other work. If you have triple-decker boards, always use the middle board first so that each board will be exposed for as long as possible. Try to write example programs or subprograms in one continous piece. Finally, I find it helpful to reserve the far right-hand board as a 'scratch paper' for test examples or questions that come up during lecture.

Copy examples from your notes.

When I started to teach I was convinced that any teacher worth her salt could wing it when it came to writing programs in class. Ah, the pride that goeth before a fall! Nowadays, I try to be perfectly frank with my students in admitting a total inability to think on my feet. You may feel silly about copying simple program examples, but trivial errors (like using the wrong identifier) are easy to make, and hopelessly confuse students who are trying to take notes, listen, and think at the same time. Once students are confused by an instructor's mistake they tend to go into autopilot, and are lost for the rest of the lecture.

Require that reading be completed before class.

In my experience, the stronger students—who might be expected to follow the lecture even without advance preparation—do the reading in advance, while weaker students compound their difficulty by avoiding assigned reading. Absolutely requiring that reading be completed before the relevant material is discussed in class helps guarantee a minimum baseline of understanding. I think that this is probably the single most important ingredient for a successful lecture to a large group.

Avoid giving assignments that involve material that has not been presented yet.

Again, this bit of advice is for the benefit of the weaker students. I've found that students who have come to expect that they won't understand the content of an assignment tend not to read it until the last minute. In the long run this increases load on staff and machines.

Don't give comprehensive exams on material that hasn't been reinforced by a completed and graded assignment.

This will usually mean that tests should involve material that was covered in class at least a week previously. I find that this approach allows harder and more comprehesive tests, yet is fairer to the students.

Give weekly assignments.

Weekly assignments help ensure that students actually work regularly, and thus allow a greater workload. It does not mean that assignments must be small, though. Large (i.e. two-three week assignments) should be turned into multi-part homeworks by requiring weekly milestones.

Give an early assignment that involves a substantial amount of typing.

Students are intimidated by the size of programs. I find that giving them a program that is long because of straightforward, but repetitive, code segments is a simple, but effective, confidence builder. I also prefer that they learn the price of waiting until the last minute (e.g. terminal room jams) early in the term.

Post sample examinations, and executable versions of required programs. Print solutions to exams and homeworks after they're completed.

This suggestion is just intended to help maintain the minimum baseline of understanding.

Encourage students to meet other students.

I was amazed to find the extent to which students remained anonymous in large classes. I allow a minute in each of the first few classes for 'neighbor' introductions. I also require that any student who asks for help in the terminal room know the name of the person sitting next to her. Why bother? Because students prefer not being isolated, and a happy class is much easier to teach.

Encourage students to work together.

It is my unfailing experience that, whether or not it is permitted, the better students invariably work together. I usually computer-generate voluntary study groups after the first midterm (two better students are matched with three poorer students). Individual face-to-face grading ensures that students have actually learned the material.

Use the computer to make class more personal.

Don't just rely on the computer as a machine for doing homework. Developing a community atmosphere in class helps overcome natural student resentment of courses that are required, overcrowded, or underfunded. Some of the suggestions given below require getting some information from students at first login, including name, major, birthday, phone number, first language, etc.

- To improve contact with the instructor: require student mail, create an anonymous 'suggest' or 'complain' command, allow voting on class issues, have a program automatically generate birthday greetings.
- To improve contact with the staff: create on-line staff biographies, put schedules on line, advertise under-attended sections.
- To improve contact between students: have a program generate special interest groups or study groups based on residence, major, first language, etc. Generate study or project groups based on class performance (give each group a mix of student ability). Support an electronic class bulletin board.

Don't give yourself unnecessary aggravation.

There is a difference between being conscientious and being masochistic. Some hints for reducing grief:

- Put your effort into making exams and assignments fair—not in arguing about their grading. Let your staff take care of as many disputes as possible.
- Don't take responsibility for things that are beyond your control. Sympathize with students about the inadequacy of computer facilities—don't apologize for them.
- If office hours make you uncomfortable, but impromptu consulting is something you enjoy, hold office hours in the terminal room.

A Note on the Chapter Highlights

This section contains a chapter-by-chapter outline for *Oh! Pascal!* Here are some general suggestions for using the text effectively:

- Give explicit assignments. This means requesting required reading, but may also imply specifically excluding material that is beyond the scope of your course. The text has too broad a range of coverage for directions like 'read the first five chapters.'
- Don't try to teach everything in the book; I certainly don't. Bear in mind that *Oh! Pascal!* is written for a wide range of students and courses, and that some details are included almost solely for reference. Many sections and examples can be omitted without making your course less challenging or effective.
- Try to introduce material in chapter order. The optional and 'discursive' sections can be introduced out of order, of course, but the main sections intentionally try to reinforce material from previous chapters. As I've said elsewhere, it may seem weird to teach **for** and **case** before **if** and **while**, but it works, so give it a try. Don't worry—you won't run out of material if you delay introducing *booleans* until the fifth week.
- The material is paced at roughly a chapter per week. In my thirty-hour, fifteen-week course I cover eleven or twelve chapters in about ten weeks, with the remainder reserved for more elaborate projects with arrays. Syntax is covered slowly because many programming concepts are introduced as they become applicable. The book is less effective, and the course less interesting, if the instructor tries to 'get the Pascal out of the way' first.
- The chapters are set up to allow a 'hard, easy' presentation. In general, the first section of each chapter contains the detailed new material, while subsequent sections allow some breathing space for consolidation.

Finally, let me stress the importance of selectively passing over some portions of the text. For instance, certain hard examples (palindromic numbers, gerund conversion) are primarily intended to enrich the text for the benefit of better students, and may be too difficult to be effectively discussed in class. I sometimes have a TA run an 'advanced' section to discuss such topics.

Chapter One

To Highlight...

Using a text editor for mail and simple programs. Importance of comments, declaring variables of different types, echoing input. *write* and *writeln* provide a good first example of arbitrary (to the student) Pascal 'rules.' The arithmetic operators, particularly **div** and **mod**, since they'll be useful for assignments that involve breaking up numbers or converting *char* input. Compile-time error messages. I recommend assigning programs that are easy—even trivial arithmetic will do—but numerous, because from the student's point of view, dealing with the system will be the main problem.

Less Important...

Syntax charts, semicolons, elaborate explanations of type checking. Don't belabour the difference between *read* and *readln* (I usually wait a few weeks, then refer back to an example like the one on page 15). Output format, field widths, and *real* numbers.

Some Suggestions...

Underline reserved words on the blackboard. Discuss specific error messages in class. Encourage experimentation to determine simple rules (e.g. *write* vs. *writeln*). As mentioned above, I think that requiring a variety of simple programs is more important than trying for hard code—at this stage of the game, I prefer three 10-line programs to one 30-line 'monster.'

I usually leave discussions of computer hardware until the latter part of the term, although I will discuss the operating system briefly. The brief exposition in the Introduction answers most questions.

I try to tread a careful path between ignoring system and Pascal details, and harping on them. Although I would like to minimize the number of details that novice students must learn, I realize that eventually they have to get used to dealing with system messages and documentation. I think that 'mail' is a suitable system command to explore, while **div** and **mod** are good examples of Pascal detail.

I've found that comparing a computer to the telephone provides a useful analogy for total novices. The dial tone is like the login message, the dial is a limited keyboard, a completed call compares to a successful command, and the familiar 'I'm sorry, your call cannot be completed as dialed' pairs with an incorrectly entered command as a syntactic error. Best of all, a wrong number—incorrect but successful—corresponds to a semantic error.

Numbered Exercises

Lecture Review Sections: 1−13, 15, 18−22. Discuss 31.
Problem Solving Sections: 13−14, 16, 23−24, 26−27.
As Homework Problems: 13-14, 23, 26−27.

Chapter Two

To Highlight...

Meaningful identifiers (I'll often play a recording of the Abbott and Costello *Who's On First?* routine in class—it's usually available at airport gift stores). Form and evaluation of expressions, parentheses, type clashes. Assignment statements, legal and illegal. Form and meaning of function calls (i.e. as representing values, rather than changing values). Although I may mention all the standard functions briefly, I mainly deal with *sqr* and *sqrt* (for type examples) and *ord* and *chr* (for use in homework assignments).

Less Important...

Operator precedence. I usually give only a brief mention to constants at this point. Fixed-point notation is entirely optional. Functions besides *ord* and *chr* are covered briskly. I want students to begin thinking about problem solving (hence the elegance section), but I don't really discuss it in class yet. I cover this chapter very quickly, since much of its material is either conceptually simple (like the explanation of expressions or arithmetic operators), or will mainly be useful for later reference (like the constant definition rules, or the function definitions).

Some Suggestions...

There is usually some confusion about the exact time of evaluation of function calls and assignments. Questions like 2−18 (rewriting two consecutive assignments as a single statement) are good 'synthesis' problems. As with the first chapter, I would recommend focusing briefly on some likely run-time or compile-time errors and error messages.

For homework at this point, I like to assign programs that involve translations between numbers and characters. I don't want to get bogged down in syntax or weird I/O rules, but I do feel that students need some practice with solving technical problems. Again, I prefer a variety of small programs to one large one.

Numbered Exercises

Lecture Review Sections: 1−15, 18−20, 26−28. Discuss 30.
Problem Solving Sections: 15−17, 21−25, 27−29.
As Homework Problems: 16, 24, 28.

Chapter Three

To Highlight...

The idea of a procedure or function. Using value parameters. Correspondence between arguments and parameters. Differences between value and variable parameters, and the use of variable parameters. Using driver programs to test subprograms. Ease of rewriting a small program as a subprogram. Introduction to modular thinking—subdividing problems.

Less Important...

Don't beat scope to death. I try to avoid scope problems, especially by not using side-effects. I rarely deal with subprograms inside subprograms at this point either. I focus more on quick outlines than on top-down/stepwise refinement per se (more useful starting in the next chapter).

Some Suggestions...

This is a difficult chapter no matter how it is sliced. Because of many requests, I have consolidated material (procedures, functions, and parameters) from three different chapters of the first edition. However, I teach under the assumption that the material introduced in Chapter 3 (unlike the topics of other chapters) should not, will not, and cannot be mastered in real time. I assume that correct use of parameters, in particular, will require continuous reinforcement over the next few weeks.

I don't think it's advisable to get carried away with motivating parameters and subprograms. Remember that the student's main problems are with the mechanics of declaration and use. Give them plenty of practice in deciding what to use, and actually making the declarations. Complicated algorithms, or long code segments, tend to make students look for the easy way out in minimizing subprogram usage. I usually give an assignment that involves turning programs written earlier into subprograms in a large program.

An idea for introducing parameters in class: Frisbees carrying values (seal the value-parameter frisbees in Saran Wrap). Another approach: have students with identical names act as like-named variables to help establish scope rules (I set up a living version of the block diagram on page 70). My most practical suggestion: split the introduction over two days (end of one lecture, beginning of the next), rather than putting it all in one. Everybody will seem much smarter in the second class.

Numbered Exercises

Lecture Review Sections: 1–18, 22, 24. Discuss 28–30.
Problem Solving Sections: 18–21, 23, 25–27.
As Homework Problems: 18, 21, 25.

Chapter Four

To Highlight...

Statements—procedure calls, input/output, assignments. Compound and empty statements (although they won't be useful for another ten minutes). Finally, syntax of the **for** statement. Number of iterations, evaluation of starting and final value on entry to the statement. Examples of **for** statements controlling empty statements, procedure calls, compound statements, including buggy examples. Start to use more pseudocode and stepwise refinement. Cover a number-averaging procedure in class.

Less Important...

The detailed rules on the counter (although they should be mentioned). Complicated nesting—save this for examples in the next (**case**) chapter. I think that the examples in the text (drawing bars, printing patterns, finding Fibonaccis) are useful to read, but are less important to emphasize in class. The relevance of the discussion of defensive programming and snapshot procedures depends on the current assignment—it's useful if they're required. I may reserve this discussion until I deal with stub programming and commenting-out code in Chapter 5.

Section 4−2 (an early introduction to arrays) appears in response to a small, but vocal, demand. Besides its obvious application to more scientifically oriented classes, I think this section will appeal to students who know BASIC and are in a hurry to program.

Some Suggestions...

Try to motivate all of Pascal's statements before starting out, giving an advance picture of what can be expected in the next few weeks. I try very hard to make all the **for** examples take shape as procedures or functions, and continually hammer away at the choice of subprogram, and of value or variable parameter. Remember, this is still a big technical problem for the student. I want them to practice these basic skills on relatively easy algorithms.

As a rule, I try to chart a regular course when I introduce statements: first the syntax, then examples of the basic single-action case, then a compound statement, then a degenerate case or two, and finally a couple of buggy examples. This is the first lecture. The next lecture is consolidation—stating and solving problems that require the new statement.

Numbered Exercises

Lecture Review Sections: 1−10, 10, 15, 19, 21. Discuss 25.
Problem Solving Sections: 10−18, 20, 22−24, esp. 10−15, 18−20.
As Homework Problems: 11, 13, 17, 20, 23.

Chapter Five

To Highlight...

case statement syntax. Type of case expression and constants, need for complete constant list. First intentional example of the empty statement. Nested **case** statements, **case** statements inside **for** loops. The idea of brute-force solutions. Using **case** for counting (as in *CountDigits*, page 144).

Less Important...

The random number generator and bar graphing examples; these are good if an assignment draws on them, but may be too involved to be class examples. The embedded word example is the first of a number of fairly hard text problems, intended solely for the better students and not discussed in class. The section on analysing algorithms is entirely new, and should probably be returned to after arrays are presented. It is included here because I wanted to get some of the terms on the table for the benefit of the better students.

Some Suggestions...

My programming assignments jump in length at about this time. To help support them, I recommend discussing mechanical methods of dealing with long programs, in particular, any special editor commands that will help in copying or transfer of long code segments.

I also focus on some of the more general programming considerations that have been included, but basically glossed over, in the past few chapters. From Chapter 3 comes top-down design and stepwise refinement, and the first comments about program modularity. Chapter 4's discussion of defensive programming—extensive commenting of subprograms, and the use of snapshot procedures—is mentioned in class, but dealt with mainly in sections and the terminal room.

Chapter 5 provides stub programming. I go over the development of stub procedures in class, and require that they be used in an assignment's Week One milestone. I encourage drafting, but commenting out, of partially ready code sections for a simple reason—many students type badly. I want them to get some of the raw volume of character entry out of the way early.

Numbered Exercises

Lecture Review Sections: 1−12, 12, 17, 19, 23, 25, 32−34. Discuss 35.
Problem Solving Sections: 13−24, 27−28.
As Homework Problems: 14−15, 21, 23, 27.

Chapter Six

To Highlight...

Relational operators, then *boolean* operators. Evaluating *boolean* expressions (mentioning full evaluation). The **if** statement alone, and then with an **else** part. **if** statements in conjunction with **for** statements.

I describe simple set usage, but don't dwell on it. I do focus on embedded debugging tools, carrying over from the last chapter's discussion of stub programming and commenting out code. The change-making program (185) and stolen gold program (187) are good for contrasting sequential and **if** statements.

Less Important...

Changing the association of the **else** part (I have almost never had to do this in programming). Precedence of *boolean* operators (use parentheses instead). Truth tables and transformation laws. The embedded word and bowling programs continue the series of relatively hard non-mathematical programs aimed more at the better student than at the class; likewise the discussion of exhaustive search and solution spaces. I rarely dwell on the relative merits (especially efficiency) of equivalent, but differently nested, code segments.

Some Suggestions...

I usually describe **if** briefly at the beginning of class, but I'll always have a full discussion of *boolean* expressions before going into examples of the statement. Since I expect students to have done the reading by the time they come to class, I assume that the general need for *booleans* is already motivated.

As with the other control statements, my first lecture on the **if** contains a straightforward progression of examples: is a number in a range? is it in, or out? if it's out, why? I repeatedly add **ands** or **else** parts to the most recent example. At this point, I'm more interested in having students see the progression from a simple bit of code to a complicated sequence, and less worried about presenting and explaining different complicated segments.

For the second lecture I start to pose and solve problems. A more mathematically-inclined course may introduce some concepts, like counters and accumulators, that are more traditionally associated with the conditional loops.

The discussion of embedded debugging tools (205−206) is new in this edition. Although I haven't yet modified my own programming assignments to require their use, I probably will in the near future.

Numbered Exercises

Lecture Review Sections: 1−18, 22, 36, 38. Discuss 39.
Problem Solving Sections: 18−21, 23−27, 29−32, 35, 37.
As Homework Problems: 19−20, 28, 30, 34.

Chapter Seven

To Highlight...

Need for conditional loops in completing the set of Pascal statements. Basic loop syntax. Entry/exit conditions, the necessity of approaching the exit condition. Implausible exit or entry conditions, convenience of *boolean* functions. Knowing exactly why you have left a loop.

Basic loop applications, using sentinels, counters, and accumulators. Program robustness (both with **if** and loops). Entry, exit, and off-by-one errors, loop bugs as described on 248−249. General loop processing models (as on 250). Heavy emphasis on pseudocode and stepwise refinement.

Less Important...

I usually don't dwell on **repeat** vs. **while** at the time, but when I choose one for an example, I think out loud about why I want one or the other.

Recursion is introduced in 7−3 for convenience, because the presentation doesn't require any additional material. I would only introduce it at this time in a high-powered course, but I would recommend preserving the format of the presentation (esp. the sequence of examples) if and when you do get into recursion.

Some Suggestions...

Although *boolean* expressions were introduced in the previous chapter, I still pay a lot of attention to using them properly. In developing examples, I'll often leave a blank space where the *boolean* or relational operator is supposed to go, and return to it after dealing with the loop body. I encourage pencil and paper testing of boundary conditions for loop entrance or exit, and reassure my students that I, too, check my code like this.

I focus heavily on semantic bugs. I generally develop the summing-loop bugs one at a time, wringing my hands as I try desperately to get my code right. 'Where am I on loop exit?' bugs get a similar treatment. I repeatedly stress the correct syntax of my semantically incorrect code, as well as the sometimes-correct output of code known to contain special-case bugs.

Numbered Exercises

Lecture Review Sections: 1−12, 13, 28−29. Discuss 35.
Problem Solving Sections: 14−17, 19−21, 24, 29.
As Homework Problems: 14−15, 18, 21, 25−26, 30.

Chapter Eight

To Highlight...

General motivation of text processing vs. number crunching. Some discussion of the range and importance of text-oriented programs (including text editors, most business data processing, interpreters and compilers, etc.).

Review *read* and *readln*, and introduce *eof* and *eoln*. Emphasize the basic doubly-nested **while** loop model for text processing. Apply variations of the basic model to a variety of examples. I find that programs can start to require non-trivial algorithms at this point, and I continue a heavy emphasis on examples that need stepwise refinement. The new software engineering material of section 10−1 is appropriate here. Since I work on UNIX, I introduce input and output redirection now.

While earlier chapters have paid considerable attention to debugging, I now recommend shifting the focus to testing. If your current assignment can use it, requiring the creation of a test suite—a collection of command-testing input files—is good.

Less Important...

Special considerations of reading numerical input should be mentioned, but I wouldn't overdo it. A lot of the craziness involved with reading numbers can be skipped. I suggest limiting discussion to the extent that your later assignments will require. The gerund conversion program is interesting for the better students, but is too hard for class. However, I strongly recommend that you introduce the material on creating and testing modules.

Section 8−2, which deals with the file window and external files, is entirely new. How important it is will depend on your programming environment. On UNIX, I can limit discussion to the file window.

Some Suggestions...

Some good example types for cementing the concepts include problems that involve skipping characters or lines (to provoke off-by-one errors and *eof* crashes), and changing the order of *read(Ch)*; *write(Ch)* and *readln*; *writeln* (to clear up lingering confusion about the difference between the input and output streams). Synchronization bugs (288) should be discussed at some point.

As mentioned above, I bring up the software engineering topics from Chapter 10 here, partially so that we can linger (and prepare for the second midterm) before moving on to structured types.

Numbered Exercises

Lecture Review Sections: 1−10, 11, 13, 19.
Problem Solving Sections: 10, 12−14, 16, 21−22.
As Homework Problems: 10, 15, 17−18, 20.

Chapter Nine

To Highlight...

Final definition of simple types and their use in programming. Enumerated ordinal types, uniqueness of constants in any given type, limits of I/O. Subrange types and rules. General desirability of enumerated types and named subranges (documentation, antibugging, etc.).

Less Important...

Pathological cases of value parameters that involve subranges. I usually assume that most student applications will be relatively straightforward. The discussion of correctness (section 9−2) is new, and can be returned to at a much later time without harm.

Some Suggestions...

This chapter is covered quickly. Since enumerated ordinal types mainly find application in larger programs, I tend to move quickly to a discussion of software engineering, as covered in Chapter 10. I steer entirely clear of problems with scope of enumerated ordinal identifiers.

Numbered Exercises

Lecture Review Sections: 1−11.

Chapter Ten

To Highlight...

Preparation for larger projects in the latter part of the term. The software life cycle, with some attention paid to each of the stages: analysis, specification, design, coding, testing, and maintenance. I put particular emphasis on problems that will develop in group work, since my course culminates in a large group project.

Less Important...

I think that going into the details of particular methodologies is of little use. Indeed, I might caution against being overly prepared for this talk. I have found out the hard way that, when a class is used to a certain amount of give and take in the development of algorithms and code, a well-prepared lecture on software engineering puts everybody to sleep. I think that a quick development of the main themes, followed by a more anecdotal discourse that relates practical experience to the points you've raised, is a more effective approach.

I ask that section $10-2$ (Meet the Types) be read, but I don't discuss it in class. My impression is that structured types are not particularly intuitive concepts for most students. I think that they understand the next few chapters better if they have an idea of what structured types are, and how they are used overall.

Some Suggestions...

There has been a tendency to focus the course quite narrowly up until now, concentrating solely on the presentation of Pascal or specific programming techniques. In the second half of the course, I start bringing in more real-world examples, so that students can see how what they've learned can be applied in a practical sense. Apropos of software engineering in particular, it's usually easy to find a software fiasco in the headlines (the new IRS tax computer, the latest multimillion dollar spreadsheet package) for illustrative purposes.

I also like to relate the computer systems that students see being advertised all around them (primarily micro systems) to the minis or mainframes they work with in class. In particular, I like to contrast the toolbox approach of UNIX-scale systems with the one-shot integrated packages that are so popular on micros. In addition, I talk about some of the economic and marketing factors that influence the development of commercial software, and compare them to software production in academic environments.

Chapter Eleven

To Highlight...
Characteristics of a legal array type definition. Distinction between subscript and element types. Size of arrays, computing subscripts. Basic locomotion through arrays, particularly with **for** loops. Some drill on alternative paths through a multi-dimensional array (e.g. row major, column major, etc.). Holding subscripts constant; building in snapshot procedures for checking subscript values.

I try to avoid making major distinctions between one, two, and n-dimensional arrays. In developing examples, I will often say 'Well, let's keep tabs on ... as well,' and add an extra set of bounds to the array type definition, and an extra **for** loop to my array-processing routines.

Strings and text processing depend on importance to your course. Relative value of string types versus plain arrays of *char*. Defining procedures for primitive operations on data structures (356−362).

Less Important...
Searching will depend on your course. I limit my discussion to linear searches, and am mainly interested in demonstrating searching bugs. However, pattern matching may be useful, depending on your assignments. See the new section 16−3, String Matching.

The new recursive array manipulation section (11−3) is obviously optional, and may be returned to later.

Some Suggestions...
Motivating the need for array types is a necessity. Fortunately, real life abounds with examples. As with control statements, I follow a regular method of presenting structured types: the syntax, some correct examples, some pathological examples, and some buggy examples. Basically, I try to get the motivation and ground rules out of the way in one lecture, then start stating and solving problems the next time.

In practice, I will exhaustively develop manipulation operations (centering, shifting, and the like) on one-dimensional arrays, then require that students do equivalent operations on two-dimensional arrays as part of homework. I think that problems that require close coordination between text processing loops and array processing loops are especially good for exercising the student's understanding.

An interesting way to motivate subscripts involves considering the different ways they can be used. In the presentation outlined below, each application is a slight generalization of its predecessor. We imagine that arrays keep track of values:

by sequence:
    Subscripts are used only to preserve the ordering of the first, second, etc. value of an input sequence.

by order:
    Sequences are generalized to multiple dimensions: the third seat in the second row, the fourth hour on the first day.

by coordinate:
    Order is generalized to allow abstract collections of coordinates. Subscripts indicate the element at a particular intersection of coordinates.

by relation:
    Coordinates are generalized to be meaningful relations of enumerated values, rather than coordinates of strictly ordinal sequences. We find an element by listing the unique values that

    describe it.

by attribute:

    Relations are turned inside out. We find the attributes of an element by inspecting the subscripts of its location.

Numbered Exercises

Lecture Review Sections: 1−9, discuss 24.

Problem Solving Sections: 9−10, 10, 12, 15, 17, 20.

As Homework Problems: 11−12, 14, 20−21, 23.

Chapter Twelve

To Highlight...

Methods of creation and access. Fields, basic scope rules. Complete record assignment, period notation, and the **with** statement. The concept of data structures, and practice defining data types. Problems with notation and confusing sequences of periods and square brackets. Basic record applications—a word and a number (e.g. address file, team names and scores), and a pattern and a count (e.g. a word and its length, a letter pair and its frequency). Ordering or searching arrays based on the content of a field of each element.

Less Important...

I don't find much need to dwell on the **with** statement, and record variants can be omitted entirely. As with arrays, the importance of sorting examples will depend on your class.

This is a good time to begin talking about the underlying machine—allocation of memory and limits of data storage. I also like to bring up the data typing solutions of other languages (BASIC, FORTRAN, COBOL) in contrast to Pascal.

Some Suggestions...

I believe that in many courses, the array is the last sure topic. An additional chapter (usually records or files) may be covered, but it is with the intention of allowing a complex and realistic final project. To support this goal, I think that practice in sizing up problems and defining data types is extremely important—when are records needed, when will arrays do, when are arrays of records required? Development of and comparisons between alternative type defintions (as in the alternative baseball types on page 392) are useful, and are fun in class.

Since many courses end their introduction of new Pascal at this point, what are some additional topics? One possibility is to explore sections of the text that have been skipped previously, particularly 5−2 (analysing algorithms), 7−3, 11−3, and parts of 16 (all dealing with recursion), 8−2 (the file window and external files), or 10−1 (software engineering). Another alternative is a return to the Introduction, which suggests a variety of topics in hardware and software.

For variety, I sometimes like to explore the operation and implementation of a complicated piece of software, like a spreadsheet or a drill/tutor program. Students often have difficulty recognizing that they can understand how such programs are put together; they have learned Pascal, and perhaps many programming techniques as well, but still don't realize that they now know how to write many of the programs they come into contact with.

One final suggestion is to teach another programming language— but with a twist. Instead than teaching a general-purpose language, present an extremely specialized language. I have found that text formatters (like troff, on UNIX) are ideal in this context, since they have much of the paraphenalia of conventional languages (variables, if statements, 'procedures,' and so on), but clearly suit different needs.

Numbered Exercises

Lecture Review Sections: 1−11, discuss 17.
Problem Solving Sections: 11−16.
As Homework Problems: 13−15.

Chapter Thirteen

To Highlight...

The general context: Pascal's default I/O versus I/O that is stored or directed at the system level. Various types of I/O devices. Textfiles, file parameters. Procedures *rewrite* and *reset*. Arguments to *read, readln, write* and *writeln*. Limits on file variables and parameters.

There are a small enough number of basic textfile manipulations to allow a thorough presentation, including examples of concatenation, merge, append, insertion, and comparison.

Less Important...

The importance of non-text files depends on your own assignments. I discuss their application, but don't use them in specific assignments. Redefining the standard I/O procedures for textfiles in terms of *get* and *put* makes for an interesting section, but a confusing class.

The card-finding program is too difficult for class. I keep it in the text because of the variety of data types it employs, and because it lets me develop a hard program out of an easily-stated algorithm.

The detailed digression on numbers in textfiles (442−444) is probably more useful for the TA's than for the students.

Some Suggestions...

Explaining Pascal files in the context of your local system's concept of a file is necessary. This is as good a time as any for a heart-to-heart talk about local extensions.

I would recommend that you require reading section 8−2 (the file window and external files), pages 280−286. It integrates the file window into the discussion of textfiles and has some interesting examples.

Text processing often requires a great deal of coordination between files and arrays. In practice, this is very confusing to some students. I would suggest some simple examples that involve getting line-by-line input from a file, manipulating it in an array, then printing it to a file again.

Finally, if it is appropriate for your students, this is a good time to digress into a discussion of business data processing. I try to address some of the issues that are especially relevant to business school students, including file system maintenance, security, practical limitations on storage, and space/time tradeoffs.

Numbered Exercises

Lecture Review Sections: 1−13, 13−15, 17, 22, 26. Discuss 32.
Problem Solving Sections: 15−17, 19−21, 23−31.
As Homework Problems: 18, 23, 27, 29, 31.

Chapter Fourteen

To Highlight...
Set syntax and usage rules. Comparison to **array of** *boolean*. The idea
of set-valued expressions (confusing). Set operators, and set
comparisons.

Less Important...
Depending on your course, the entire chapter is optional.

Some Suggestions...
Unless you specifically require set-oriented assignments, you may not
need them. Although there are interesting set applications, this chapter
is developed largely for the sake of completeness.

Numbered Exercises
Lecture Review Sections: 1−10, 10−12, 17, 22. Discuss 26.
Problem Solving Sections: 10−12, 14−16, 18−21.
As Homework Problems: 13, 22−24.

Chapter Fifteen

To Highlight...

The concepts of direct and indirect references (interpolating memory addresses on programmable pocket calculators is good for motivating this). Pointer type syntax. Procedure *new*, **nil** values, and what the value of a pointer might be if we could inspect it. The basic node or element, general possibilities for interconnections between nodes. Design of specific data structures by precisely defining legal interconnections. Basic operations—travelling, searching, adding, inserting, connecting. Pointers as parameters. Ease of making errors, and importance of using snapshot procedures to check the contents of pointer-based data structures. Relative advantages of array-based, file-based, and pointer-based data structures.

Less Important...

Once more, detailed coverage depends on the course. Linked lists alone are quite ambitious for any first course, while stacks make a good special project. Graphs, sparse matrices, and trees are best introduced in a limited sense, concentrating on applications of the data structure rather than on the code needed to support it.

Procedure *dispose* can be mentioned briefly, while record variants can be ignored. The keyword in context program is, of course, difficult, and is intended more for reading than for class discussion. The shorter programs (like *LinkAndEcho*, *AddPolyNamials*, and the Morse code procedure *Decode*) are short enough for a reasonable class presentation.

Some Suggestions...

Although we have forgotten it by now, the notation used for pointers is extremely confusing. This is especially true when records have only been introduced in a cursory manner. In fact, the reason I placed records before arrays in the first edition was to make sure that students learned record syntax on its own, and not as a special type of array. I recommend explaining, out loud, what is going on every time you start to jot down periods and arrows.

I have found the *Oh! Pascal!* approach to introducing pointers (by starting with pointers to simple types) useful, even though such pointers have no practical application. Overall, I caution instructors that, although one can plunge into simple pointer applications (say, using lists), one pays a price in the long run if students don't have a solid conceptual understanding of what pointers are.

I think that while it's reasonable to expect students to follow a great deal of the code in Chapter Fifteen, it is overly ambitious to expect them to be able to duplicate or originate it. In contrast to the early part of the course, when I felt that a large amount of fairly low-level practice was important, I think that high-level practice is most useful now— deciding when and where to use what data structure, rather than memorizing (because that's what they do) code for procedures like *AddAWord* (which recursively adds a string to an alphabetically-ordered binary tree).

Numbered Exercises

Lecture Review Sections: 1−10, 10−12, discuss 19.
Problem Solving Sections: 13−18.
As Homework Problems: 14−15, 17.

Chapter Sixteen

This chapter is entirely at the option of the instructor. Although it contains a fair amount of code, it is intended to provoke interest and discussion rather than programming assignments. It assumes understanding of section $5-2$ (analysing algorithms, particularly pages $154-158$).

To my mind, nothing destroys interest in the topics of Chapter 16—sorting, searching, and string matching—more rapidly than presenting them as series of algorithms and analyses. Although this may ensure adequate preparation for the Advanced Placement test, it renders an exciting sequence of innovations and discoveries insipid and lifeless.

There are a variety of ways to enliven the presentation of programming algorithms. First, characterize the algorithm's historical place. How was the problem dealt with before the new algorithm was invented? Did any change in technology make a new method work? Did the creation of a new computer application make a better algorithm essential? Has the new algorithm made any new applications possible?

Second, focus on the algorithm's creator. Does he have any other claim to fame? What was he looking for in the first place? How did he approach the problem? How else might have he proceded? Did other researchers get thrown off by following blind alleys?

Third, one can speculate about the genesis of the algorithm, or the difficulty of its creation. Why did so-and-so get an algorithm named after him? After all, it seems so obvious now! What was the special insight that helped bring this algorithm to light? Or was it the result of applying a more general trick ('use randomness,' or 'take bigger steps') that had been successful elsewhere?

As a final point, I have no suggestions to make on the Appendix (which discusses some of the more obscure points of Pascal). Somehow, I have never had occassion to draw attention to its contents.

A Note on the Chapter Review/Quiz Questions

This section contains a large number of questions grouped by chapter. Questions for the first eleven chapters (through arrays) are fairly exhaustive—forty to fifty questions per chapter are supplied, many with Pascal code. The remaining chapters are treated more briefly, since questions involving code tend to run quite long. Each chapter's questions include:

Understanding code ... These are short, easy-to-grade questions that concentrate on interpreting programs, and recognizing correct syntax and semantics. They are similar to the *Self-Check* questions that appear in the text. Although I haven't prepared them as such, they're suited to be multiple-choice questions.

Short responses ... These questions all involve brief prose answers, and are best used on self-graded quizzes.

Write a program that ... These questions all call for relatively short code segments.

When answers are included, they are supplied between square brackets in bold type.

Questions tend to be drill-type problems that focus on the current chapter, rather than being comprehensive. A quiz suitable for a section might include a half-dozen 'understanding code' questions, two or three 'short responses,' and one or two 'write a program's. Many of the problems are useful as short introductory examples for lecture or section.

Most of the problem types are probably familiar, but some may not be. In particular:

- **Here's the input, what's the output?** Questions of this sort can be done mechanically, grinding one data item at a time through the mill, but carry the penalty of excessive time consumption. Better students will translate the Pascal into pseudocode, and can carry out the intent of the code more quickly.
- **Here's the output, what's the input?** I think this is the ideal problem type—hard to do, but easy to grade. Again, the student has to figure out what the code does; essentially 'deprogramming' the problem.
- **Rewrite this code segment without using ...** These questions require transformation of code from one set of control statments to another.

In the later chapters, I have supplied many short programs that can be used as you like: provide input or output, ask what the program does, introduce simple bugs and have the student spot them, or ask that small modifications be made.

A class of problems that has been used with success at Berkeley, but which is not represented here, involve supplying the student with the listing of an ongoing project (10–20 pages), and asking for modifications, debugging, shortcomings of proposed test data, etc. This approach allows a realistic test of programming skill, is relatively easy to grade, and (since the listing is made available before the exam) is perceived by the students as a fair test. However, the overhead of devising and coding such a project is high. Maybe next year...

Chapter One

Understanding code ...

1 • Find three legal identifiers:

>   HABIT   3rdTry   for   begin   .asleep
>   Awake   for_nothing   −zero   one   6.3

2 • Are any of these legal Pascal?

>   {program TrialAndError (input, output);}
>
>   {program TrialAndError (input, output);}
>   program TrialAndError (input, output);
>
>   {{{ This is a comment. }}}

3 • Is this a legal program?

>   program Testing (input, output);
>   begin
>   end.

4 • The standard input and output procedures are ...?

5 • Show the output of these statements. Print a carriage return as <cr>, and a space as _.

>   write ('Go, Bob, Go');
>   writeln ('Go, Bob, Go');
>   writeln (1+1);
>   writeln ('1', −1);
>   writeln ('''');
>   writeln (''   );
>   writeln (', '', ');
>   writeln ('D', '1+2');
>   writeln ('D', 1+2);
>   writeln ('H', ','',' ');

6 • How do you print a carriage return?

7 • True or false: A carriage return may be part of a *writeln*? A *write*? A comment?

8 • Is this correct Pascal? Fix the error if there is one.

>   writeln
>   ; writeln

9 • What is the output of this program segment? Show a blank line as <blank>.

>   writeln;
>   write ('A short test ');
>   write ('to make sure ');
>   writeln ('that you know ');
>   write ('all about the ');
>   writeln ('very important ');
>   writeln;
>   writeln ('output procedures. ');

10 • Write these values as Pascal reals.

−37	.000395	.721
8.750	−832.001	983.2904
484,783	662	10^9

11 • Is this legal Pascal?

    var High: integer;
        Low: real;
        Medium: integer;

12 • Match the variables with the values they can represent. (Some values may be illegal.) Assume these declarations:

    var IntVal: integer; ChVal: char; ReVal: real;

−7E−12	ht		.782
−14	−5E+5.0	13.E+19	F
7,382	77.7E−77	0	0.0
−21.8	.8E5	−	8

13 • What is the last value read, and the value about to be read, for each of these statements? Show a blank as <blank>, and the start of the next line as <start>. Assume that this variable declaration has been made:

    var Ca, Cb, Cc, Cd, Ce, Cf: char;

and that input to *each* statement is: 54321

        read (Cc);
        read (Cc); read (Ca);
        read (Cf, Ce, Cd);
        read (Ce, Ca, Cd, Cb, Cc);
        read (Ca, Cb, Cc, Cd, Ce, Cf);
        readln;
        read (Cb); readln (Ca);
        readln (Cf);
        readln (Ca, Cb, Cc);
        readln (Ca, Cb, Cc, Cd, Ce);

14 • Which of these statements are true?

A.   The carriage return is always read as a blank.
B.   If the carriage return is read and immediately echoed, a return will be printed.
C.   The carriage return cannot be read.

15 • What is the value of each variable after the statements shown below? What value is about to be read? If a statement causes a crash, which value created the problem? Assume these variable definitions:

    var Num1, Num2: integer; Ch1, Ch2: char;

Assume that the input to *each* statement is: 739 T52Z
There is a single space between the 9 and T.

        read (Num2, Num1);   read (Num1, Ch2);
        read (Ch2, Num2);   read (Num2, Ch2, Num1);
        read (Ch2, Ch1, Num2);   read (Num1, Ch2, Ch1, Num2);
        read (Ch2);   readln (Num2);
        readln (Ch2);   readln;

16 • Suppose that A, B, and C are integer-valued variables. Which of these is likely to be the correct output of the statements below? [**B (looking for right-alignment, vs. centered or left-aligned)**]

        writeln (A, B, C);
        writeln (C, A, B);

A.
| 1245 | 4645987 | 6 |
| 6 | 1245 | 4645987 |

B.
| 1245 | 4645987 | 6 |
| 6 | 1245 | 4645987 |

C.
| 1245 | 4645987 | 6 |
| 6 | 1245 | 4645987 |

17 • Which of these are legal Pascal?

```
writeln ('Here is
    a long sentence. ');

writeln ('Here is
a long sentence. ');

writeln ('Here is ');
    ('a long sentence. ');
```

Short responses ...

18 • Describe in words, or with a syntax chart, the rules for creating an identifier.

19 • What is a reserved word? Why must reserved words be treated specially?

20 • Write a syntax chart for your name that allows the option of a) a skipped middle name; b) a middle name *or* middle initial.

21 • What are the purpose of comments?

22 • Must a program have input? Output? Discuss briefly.

23 • What steps do you have to take in writing and running a program?

24 • What is the difference between program *compilation* and program *execution*?

25 • What is the cursor? Where is it after a *write*? *writeln*? *read*? *readln*?

26 • Why are variables necessary?

27 • What is a prompt? When is it needed?

28 • When does type checking occur? Why?

29 • What is the difference between *real* and *integer* values?

30 • What is a type clash? Give an example.

31 • What does it mean to say that Pascal is a free-format language? What is the purpose of indenting statements?

32 • What's wrong with this program?   [**no prompt**]

```
program Double (input, output);
    var Number: integer;
begin
    read (Number);
    writeln ('Twice that number is:  ', Number*2)
end.
```

33 • What is a syntax bug? When is it found?

34 • What is a semantic bug? When is it found?

35 • What is a listing? How do you get one?

36 • What is the difference between compile-time and run-time errors? Give an example.

37 • What is documentation? Why is it necessary?

Write a program that ...

38 • Write a program that does nothing.

39 • Write a program that prints three blank lines.

40 • Write a program that reverses three input letters.

41 • Write a program that prints a real value with its whole and fractional part reversed.

42 • Write a program that prints the sum of five input values.

43 • Write a program that prints a square. A triangle.

44 • Write a program that reads two *real* values and prints their difference, then reads two *integer* values and prints their product.

45 · Write a program that computes a price, including sales tax.

46 · Write a program that adds the first value on three successive lines of input.

47 · Write a program that adds the first value on the first line of input to the second value on the second line and the third value on the third line.

48 · Write a program that multiplies the second value on three successive lines of input.

49 · Write a program that reads a letter grade (followed by a plus sign, minus sign, or space), and an *integer* test score, then prints them in reverse.

50 · Write a program that reads a date printed in European order (30,3,85) and prints it in American order (3/30/85).

Chapter Two

Understanding code ...

1 • Which of these are valid assignments?

```
1 + 3 := X;              Temp = Temp + 1;
X := Y := Z;             Temp := (Temp) * 3;
X + 2 := 5;              Y := .35;
X := 2.5 X 7;            Monogram := 'PH';
Percent := 10%;          Three := ((2)) + Two;
```

2 • Which of these expressions are always legal? Sometimes legal? Never legal? Why?

```
1+1   1+A   'A'+1   A−B   'A'−B   '1'+2   A   'B'   A/B   A*3
```

3 • State each of these as a Pascal expression:

```
negative 7 times the variable Number
the character that represents the number 8
the integer value 8
the real representation of 8
the character that represents the multiplication sign
the difference of 14 and 3
```

4 • Suppose that Ch represents a digit character. Write an expression that equals the numerical value Ch represents.

5 • Rewrite using **div** or **mod** as appropriate: [**A div B, A mod B**]

```
trunc (A/B)
A − (trunc (A/B) * B)
```

6 • Rewrite without using **div** or **mod**:

```
A div B
A mod B
```

7 • Evaluate these expressions:

```
25 mod 5        10 mod 9        5 mod 5         5 mod 12
25 div 5        10 div 9        5 div 5         5 div 12
25.0 / 5        25 / 5          25 / 5.0        1 * 1.0
```

8 • Show the following operators in order of their precedence:

```
+   *   div   −   mod   /
```

9 • Define constants that represent *pi*, your name, the value zero, this year, a negative number.

10 • Find the bug:

```
program Test (input, output);
const AGE = 19;
begin
    writeln ('If you''re not 19 enter the proper age.');
    readln (AGE);
    writeln ('Your age is:', AGE)
end.
```

11 • Which of these definitions are legal?

```
const PRESSURE = 1.39E−07:
      THIRD = 1/3;
      NAME = 'ILANA';
      INITIAL = 'D';
      NINESQUARE = sqr (9);
      AGE = User {variable to be entered by program user.}
```

12 • Print the values. Use an underline to show blank spaces.

    10:4
    1/1:1:3
    1.0:5:1
    10.0:5
    10.0:5:3

13 • Suppose that grade point averages are printed to three decimal places. Write a statement that prints the real variable GPA to this accuracy.

14 • Write an expression that represents the fourth root of the value Rootless. The eighth root.

15 • Write an expression that represents the value Low raised to the High power.

16 • Store prices are usually written to two decimal places. Write the value of the variable Stock in this way.

17 • Fix the bug:

    writeln ('Enter a value in dollars and cents. ');
    readln (Value);
    round (Value);
    writeln ('To the nearest dollar, that amount was: $', Value);

18 • Write these assignments in Pascal:

    Nature gets the natural log of 2
    Cubic represents the square root of 7
    Positive is assigned the absolute value of -19
    Start is given the character before 'a' in the computer's collating sequence
    Whole gets 5.76 rounded to the closest whole number
    Full is assigned the integer part of 5.76

19 • Which of these expressions are always correct Pascal? Sometimes correct? Never correct?

    round (X)   trunc (5)   succ (X)   chr (255)
    round ('X')   trunc (X+3)   succ ('X')   chr (ord ('X'))
    pred (5)   trunc (X+3.0)   ord (T)   sqrt (NumberValue)
    succ (9)   round (4/2)   ord ('0')   succ ('Z')

20 • Assume that Value is a variable of type *char*. Rewrite using the pred or succ functions, as appropriate: [**pred(Value), succ(Value)**]

    chr (ord (Value)−1)
    chr (ord (Value)+1)

21 • Assume that Value is a variable of type *char*. Rewrite these without using the pred and succ functions:

    pred (Value)
    succ (Value)

22 • Write each of these pairs of assignment statements as a single assignment. Simplify if possible:

    Age := 17 + OldAge;
    Age := NewAge − 5;   [**Age := NewAge − 5**]

    Height := 17 − Length;
    Height := 45 − Width;   [**Height := 45 − Width**]

    Test := 2 - Test;
    Test := Test * 3;   [**Test := 6 − (Test * 3)**]

    Age := (Age + 2) * 3;
    Age := Age * 4 − 9;   [**Age := 12 * Age + 15**]

```
Load := Load * 5 − 5;
Load := Load mod 5 + 7;              [Load := 7]


Class := 8 + 4 * Class;
Class := Class div 2 − 9;            [Class := 2 * Class − 5]
```

Short responses ...

23 • How do we distinguish a one-letter character variable from a value of type *char*?

24 • What's the difference between operators and operands? Give examples.

25 • What are the *real* operators? The *integer* operators? Why are there differences?

26 • What are parentheses used for in arithmetic expressions? Are they necessary?

27 • What is operator precedence? Is it necessary?

28 • What does 'mnemonic' mean? What is a mnemonic identifier?

29 • What is MAXINT?

30 • Give two reasons for defining constants instead of simply using the values they represent.

31 • What is the difference between fixed-point and floating-point notation? Give examples of each.

32 • What is the difference between the *round* and *trunc* functions?

33 • What is a 'collating sequence?'

34 • What is a function call? An argument? A result? A result-type? Give examples.

35 • What is a type clash? Give examples.

36 • What is an uninitialized variable?

Write a program that ...

37 • Write a program or code segment that tries to print the number after MAXINT.

38 • Write a program or code segment that reverses a three-digit number read in as an integer.

39 • Write a program or code segment that prints the last three digits of a six-digit number.

40 • Write a program or code segment that prints the first three digits of a six-digit number.

41 • Write a program or code segment that reads as input a number of days, then prints the same value in weeks and sevenths of a week. (weeks and 52nds of a year.)

42 • Write a program or code segment that reads a number of weeks as a *real*, then prints the number to the nearest day. (hours to nearest minute, days to nearest hour and minute.)

43 • Write a program or code segment that converts temperature from Farenheit to Celsius (Celsius to Farenheit) using the conversion formula C = 5/9 (F−32) (F = (9/5 C) + 32).

44 • Write a program or code segment that reads an *integer*, then prints the number that follows it. Assume that the last number in the sequence is followed by the first number. Sequences are: 0−99, 3−33, 1−100.

45 • Write a program or code segment that reads a single letter, then prints the next (previous) letter in alphabetical order, with the following special rule: if the letter is 'Z' ('A'), the next (previous) letter is assumed to be 'A' ('Z').

46 • Write a program or code segment that reads an eight-digit *integer* value, then prints it out with a comma every two digits.

47 • Write a program or code segment that reads in four digits, one per line, then prints the number they represent when read vertically (upside down). (You must read the digits as characters.)

48 • Write a program or code segment that reads an eight-digit number, then prints the sum of the digits pair by pair. (You must read the digits as characters.)

49 • Write a program or code segment that computes a check digit for an eight-digit number in the following manner: the check digit is the difference of 10 and the last digit of the sum of the digits.

50 • Write a program or code segment that computes a check digit for a capital letter according to the following rule: the letter 'A' equals 1, 'B' equals 2, etc.

Chapter Three

Understanding code ...

1 • What is the correct order of these program parts?

> statements
> procedure and function declarations
> heading
> variable declarations
> constant definitions

2 • Complete this chart:

```
program A
procedure B
    function D
        begin {D}
          ..
        end; {D}
    begin {B}
      ..
    end; {B}
procedure C
    procedure E
        begin {E}
          ..
        end; {E}
    function F
        begin {F}
          ..
        end; {F}
    begin {C}
      ..
    end; {C}
begin {A}
  ..
end. {A}
```

Identifiers defined in:	Their scope is blocks:
program ?	A,B,C,D,E,F
procedure ?	B,D
procedure C	?
function D	?
procedure ?	E
function F	?

3 • Correct these calls if necessary. Assume that identifiers given in capital letters represent *integer* constants.

> procedure Test (High: integer; Low: real);

Test (10.0, 5.0);   Test (10, 5);
Test (MIDDLE, 5.3, 9);   Test (9, 8/7, EXTREME);
Test (EXTREME − MIDDLE, 1.0*3.0);

4 • Correct these calls if necessary. Assume that identifiers given in capital letters represent constants.

> procedure Exam (var Start: integer; Finish: integer);

Exam (5, 10);   Exam (MIDDLE, EXTREME);
Exam (Trial, 10/5);   Exam (trunc (4/2), MIDDLE);
Exam (Trial, MIDDLE − EXTREME);

5 • Correct these calls if necessary. Assume that identifiers given in capital letters represent constants.

       procedure Check (First, Second: char);

    Check ('AB');   Check ('A', 1);
    Check ('A' 'B');   Check (A, B);
    Check (1, 2);

6 • In the following calls, decide if the arguments are intended for a) value parameters, b) variable parameters, or c) value or variables parameters. Assume that identifiers given in capitals represent constants.

    Call (17, 83);   Hear (TEST, PRIME);
    Find (Starter);   Lose (Start + Finish);
    Involve ('A', 'B');   Use (1, 2);

7 • Find the bug:

```
procedure Test (var High: real; Low: char);
    var High: real;
        Low: integer;
    begin
        High := High/2;
        Low := 2* Low
    end;
```

8 • Fix the bug, if absolutely necessary:

```
function Low: integer; (Start, Finish: real);
function Test: real;
function Exam ( ): char;
function Check: real;
function Trial (Start: integer; Finish: integer);
```

9 • Here's the input: −23   What's the output? [**23** <cr> **−23**]

```
program Absolute (input, output);
var Digit: integer;
function HardWay (Number: integer): integer;
    begin
        Number := sqr (Number);
        HardWay := trunc (sqrt (Number))
    end;
procedure EasyWay (var Number: integer);
    begin
        Number := abs (Number)
    end;
begin
    readln (Digit);
    writeln (HardWay (Digit));
    EasyWay (Digit);
    writeln (0 − Digit)
end.
```

10 • What's the output? [3   <cr>   **10** **3** **c** **a**]   Here's the input:

        a7
        8
        6

```
program DazedAndConfused (input, output);
var The, When:  integer;
    Breaks,Levee:  char;
procedure BlackDog (var EverMore: integer; MistyTop: char);
   begin
      readln (EverMore);
      EverMore := EverMore + ord (MistyTop) - ord ('a')
   end;
procedure StairWay (var Heaven: integer);
   begin
      BlackDog (Heaven,'b');
      Heaven := Heaven div 2;
      writeln (Heaven)
   end;
begin
   readln (Breaks,The);
   When := 6;
   Levee := 'c';
   BlackDog (When,Levee);
   StairWay (The);
   writeln (When, The, Levee, Breaks)
end.
```

11 • What are the types of the input values this program requires?

```
program Fastcars (input, output);
var Ferrari:  integer;
    Maserati:  char;
    Jaguar:  real;
procedure SkidMark (Lotus: char; var Maserati: integer);
   var Ferrari:  char;
       Jaguar:  integer;
   begin
      readln (Lotus, Ferrari);
      writeln ('Go on pick one more car.');
      readln (Maserati, Jaguar)
   end;
begin
   writeln ('How much would you pay for a Jaguar?');
   readln (Jaguar);
   SkidMark (Maserati, Ferrari);
   readln (Ferrari, Maserati)
end.
```

12 • What was the input of program *FunnyStuff*? [a] Its output is:

```
d
7 d
```

```pascal
program FunnyStuff (input, output);
const DIGIT = 7;
var Letter: char;
    NewLetter: integer;
procedure ConvertOnce (var Ch: char);
  const DIGIT = 3;
  begin
    Ch := chr (ord (Ch) + DIGIT)
  end;
function ConvertTwice (Ch: char):integer;
  const MAKEDIFFICULT = 4;
  begin
    ConvertTwice := ord (Ch) − ord ('a') + MAKEDIFFICULT
  end;

begin
  readln (Letter);
  ConvertOnce (Letter);
  writeln (Letter);
  NewLetter := ConvertTwice (Letter);
  writeln (NewLetter, ' ', Letter)
end.
```

13 • What's the output? [y   −2 <cr>   n   3]

```pascal
program Phone (input, output);
const YES = 'y';
var SoreEar, Yeah: integer;
procedure LetItRing (Who: integer);
  var Hello: char;
      Yeah: integer;
  begin
    Hello := YES;
    Who := 7;
    Yeah := 9;
    writeln (Hello, Who − Yeah)
  end;
procedure SecondHour;
  var Who: char;
      CallBack: integer;
  begin
    Who := 'n';
    CallBack := 3;
    LetItRing (CallBack);
    writeln (Who, CallBack)
  end;
begin
  SoreEar := 5;
  Yeah := SoreEar − 4;
  SecondHour
end.
```

14 • Here's the input: 10000 <cr> 0.06   What's the output?

```
program RealEstate (input, output);
var FatChance, Extra: real;
procedure ActualCost (var Cost: real; View: integer);
   begin
      View := View + trunc(Cost/100);
      Cost := (View div 10) * (10 * Cost)
   end;
procedure RealtorsFee (var Fee: real; BigBucks: real);
   var Percent: real;
   begin
      readln (Percent);
      Fee := Percent * BigBucks
   end;
begin
   readln (FatChance);
   ActualCost (FatChance, 1);
   writeln (FatChance:6:2);
   RealtorsFee (Extra, FatChance);
   writeln (Extra:6:2, '    ', FatChance:6:2)
end.
```

15 • What's the bug? [**parameter Answer, in SumSquare, should be a var parameter**]

```
program SumOfSquares (input, output);
{Prints the sum of squares, and the squared sum, of any two integers.}
var Number1, Number2, Result: integer;
procedure SumSquare (Num1, Num2: integer; Answer: integer);
   begin
      Answer := sqr (Num1) + sqr (Num2)
   end;
procedure SquareSum (Num1, Num2: integer);
   begin
      writeln ('The square of the sum is', sqr (Num1 + Num2))
   end;
begin
   writeln ('Please enter two integers. ');
   readln (Number1, Number2);
   SumSquare (Number1, Number2, Result);
   writeln ('The sum of the squares is', Result);
   SquareSum (Number1, Number2)
end.
```

16 • Here's the input: 3   7   What's the output? [**3   7   5**]

```
program Surfing (input, output);
var Surfer: integer;
    Tubular, Grody: integer;
function Think (Lip, Curl: integer): integer;
   var CutBack: integer;
   begin
      CutBack := Lip + Curl;
      Think := CutBack div 2
   end;
begin
   writeln ('Please enter two integers. ');
   readln (Tubular, Grody);
   Surfer := Think (Tubular,Grody);
   writeln (Tubular,Grody,Surfer)
end.
```

Short responses ...

17 • What is modularity? Is it desirable? Why?

18 • What is the difference between a global identifier and a local identifier? Give examples.

19 • Can a program's name be used as the identifier of a local variable? A global one? Why or why not?

20 • What is identifier scope? What is the difference between scope and precedence?

21 • What is a side-effect? Give an example. Why are they banned from your programs?

22 • Is this correct Pascal? Good programming? Explain.

```
        program Test (input, output);
        var Number: integer;
        procedure Double;
           begin
                    Number := Number * 2
              end;
```

23 • What kinds of parameters are there? When should each kind be used?

24 • What is the difference between a variable parameter and a value parameter? Give an example of each in action.

25 • May a function call be an argument of a procedure or function? To what kind of parameter?

26 • Suppose that you want to write a small, but involved section of code as a subprogram. When should you probably use a function? When should you definitely use a procedure?

27 • What is stepwise refinement? Give an example.

28 • Give three reasons for using top-down design or stepwise refinement in writing programs or solving problems.

29 • What sort of program error would cause this error message?

NUMBER OF ARGUMENTS DOES NOT AGREE WITH PARAMETER LIST

30 • What sort of program error would cause this error message?

ARGUMENT TYPE NOT IDENTICAL TO TYPE OF VARIABLE PARAMETER

31 • What sort of program error would cause this error message?

EXPRESSION TYPE CLASHES WITH TYPE OF VALUE PARAMETER

32 • What sort of program error would cause this error message?

EXPRESSION MAY NOT BE ARGUMENT OF VARIABLE PARAMETER

33 • What sort of program error would cause this error message?

NOT ENOUGH ARGUMENTS TO FUNCTION "ROUNDABOUT"

Write a program that ...

34 • Write a subprogram that capitalizes (changes to lowercase) letters.

35 • Write a subprogram that changes digit characters to the numbers they represent.

36 • Write a subprogram that represents a single-digit number as the appropriate digit character.

37 • Write a subprogram that rounds its argument to the nearest 100.

38 • Write a subprogram that adds the digits of a three-digit number.

39 • Write a subprogram that returns the whole part and fractional part (to five digits) of a *real* number as *integers*.

40 • Write a subprogram that returns the remainder of the division of two *real* numbers.

41 • Write a subprogram that returns the next letter in the computer's collating sequence.

42 • Write a subprogram that takes hours and minutes as arguments, and returns seconds.

43 • Write a subprogram that returns that whole part, and remainder, of an *integer* division.

44 • Write the smallest number of subprograms needed to produce these shapes [may I recommend shapes from I Ching?].

45 • Write a subprogram that exchanges two digits.

46 • Write a subprogram that reverses a number of 3 (4, 5) digits by calling a subprogram that exchanges two digits.

47 • Write a subprogram that returns the nearest whole number greater than its *real* argument.

Chapter Four

Understanding code ...

1 • A **for** loop's counter variable must be:

> a relatively global variable
> a relatively local variable
> a parameter
> any of the above

2 • Find the bug:

```
{Add the numbers 8.0 through 23.0}
Sum := 0.0;
for Count := 8.0 to 23.0 do
    Sum := Sum + Count;
```

3 • Find the bug:

```
{Print 'Hi' as many times as a user wants, but at least once.}
for Count := 1 to Finish do begin
    writeln ('Hi');
    writeln ('Keep going? Enter a higher finish. ');
    readln (Finish)
end;
```

4 • Find the bug:

```
{Print the even numbers from 2 through 10.}
for i := 1 to 5 do begin
    i := 2 * i;
    writeln (i)
end;
```

5 • Find the bug:

```
{Find out how many times the loop executed.}
readln (Finish);
for Count := 1 to Finish do
    Something;
writeln ('The loop executed ', Finish, ' times. ');
```

6 • What's the output?

```
for i := 1 to 10 do;
    writeln ('Hi. ');
```

7 • Is this a legal Pascal program?

```
program Test (input, output);
begin
    begin
    end
end.
```

8 • Is this a legal Pascal program?

```
program Exam (input, output);
begin
    ;;; ;
    ;
end.
```

9 • The first lines of some **for** statements are shown below. How many times does each loop action take place? Assume that the following assignments have been made.

      Letter := 'J';   Number := 7;   Bound := −3;

    a) for Counter1 := 1 to Number do action;   [7]
    b) for Counter2 := 0 to Number do; action;   [0 (empty statement)]
    c) for Ch := 'C' to 'J' do action;   [8]
    d) for Index := Letter to 'J' do action;   [1]
    e) for LetCount := 'J' to pred (Letter) do action;   [0]
    f) for Number := 1 to Number do action;   [7]
    g) for Number := Number downto 1 do action;   [7]
    h) for Count := Bound to Number do action;   [11]
    i) for Bounder := 1 downto Bound do action;   [5]

10 • Here's the input: 7 9 3 8 11   What's the output? [89]

```
begin
k := 100;
for i := 1 to 5 do
   read (j);
   k := k − j;
end;
writeln (k);
```

11 • Here's the output: 95 89 86 82 80   What's the input? [5 6 3 4 2]

```
k := 100;
for i := 5 downto 1 do begin
   read (j);
   write (k − j);
   k := k − j
end;
writeln;
```

12 • Here's the output: 20 17 14 11   What's the input? [6 3]

```
read (A, B);
for Low := A downto B do
   write ((3*Low) + 2);
writeln;
```

13 • Here's the input: 5 3 9   What's the output? [12 21 33 54 87]

```
read (A, B, C);
for i := 1 to A do begin
   D := B + C;
   B := C;
   C := D;
   write (C)
end;
writeln;
```

14 • Write this nested statement as a single **for** statement:

```
for i := 2 to 4 do
   for j := 3 to 5 do
      writeln ('Hi there. ');
```

15 • What's the output? [abbcccddddeeeee]

```
for Ch0 := 'a' to 'e' do
   for Ch1 := 'a' to Ch0 do
      write (Ch0);
writeln;
```

16 • What's the output? [**aababcabcdabcde**]

```
for Ch0 := 'a' to 'e' do
    for Ch1 := 'a' to Ch0 do
        write (Ch1);
    writeln;
```

17 • What's the output? [**aaaaabbbbcccdde**]

```
for Ch0 := 'a' to 'e' do
    for Ch1 := Ch0 to 'e' do
        write (Ch0);
    writeln;
```

18 • Where's the bug? [**Sum reset to 0 each time.**]

```
{Find the average of HowMany numbers.}
readln (HowMany);
for i := 1 to HowMany do begin
    Sum := 0;  {initialize Sum}
    read (Number);  {get the number}
    Sum := Sum + Number  {add it to the running total}
end;
writeln ('The average is  , Sum/HowMany);
```

19 • What's the output? Here's the input:

```
3  7  4  2  6  0  3  5  2  4  7  4
4  9  4  1  6  2  3  4  5  9  2  3
2  7  9  1  5  8  2  5  4  1  9  8
4  7  4  2  6  0  3  5  2  4  7  4
1  9  4  1  6  2  3  4  5  9  2  3
```

```
[6   8
5   9   11
6
3   7   11
<blank>]
```

```
for i := 1 to 5 do begin
    read (j);
    for k := 1 to j do
        read (m);
    for h := 1 to (j-1) do begin
        read (m, n);
        write (m + n)
    end;
    readln;
    writeln
end;
```

Short responses ...

20 • What type can or can't a **for** loop's counter variable be?

21 • What does it mean to increment or decrement a counter variable?

22 • What does it mean to say that a **for** loop's initial value, final value, and counter variable must all have the same type? Give a legal and an illegal example.

23 • What does it mean to say that a **for** loop's counter variable must be locally declared? Give an example.

24 • In Pascal, a **for** loop counter variable's initial and final value are determined when the loop is first entered. Suppose that you didn't know this rule. Write a brief test program that would help you deduce it.

25 • What does the Pascal rule 'it is an error to make an assignment to the counter variable from within the loop's action' mean? Give an example of an illegal assignment.

26 • What is a compound statement? What is its purpose? Give an example.

27 • What is a nested statement? Give an example.

28 • What is the purpose of pseudocode? Give an example.

29 • About how long should a procedure or function be? Why?

30 • What is defensive programming? Give three examples of defensive programming techniques.

31 • What is a 'snapshot' procedure? How is it useful?

32 • A program contains the following segment of code:

```
GetInput (First, Second);
{ Print (First, Second, Third, Fourth; }
Modify (Second, Fourth);
{ Print (First, Second, Third, Fourth; }
Translate (Third, Fourth+Second);
{ Print (First, Second, Third, Fourth; }
Order (First, Third, Second, Fourth);
{ Print (First, Second, Third, Fourth; }
```

What is the purpose of the comments? Should they be removed? How are they useful?

Write a program that ...

33 • Write a program that prints the odd numbers from 11 through 23.

34 • Write a program that prints every seventh number, starting the count with 2, between 2 and 99.

35 • Write a program that prints every third capital letter, starting the count with D.

36 • Suppose that you have ten lines of input. Write a program that reads the first number on each line, then prints the sums of that many pairs of numbers from that line. For example, if your program's input starts as:

```
5 12 4 3 9 3 5 2 9 5 1 4 5 1 3 2 5 5
3 2 6 9 33 5 98 6 5 2 5 6 2
```

its output should start as:

```
16 12 8 11 6
8 42 103
```

37 • Write a program that prints a table of conversions between whole numbers of Klingons, and Tribbles. Recall that 1 Tribble equal 4.9 Klingons, plus 4. Accept as input the low and high number of Klingons for the table.

38 • Write a program that prints every pattern of the form 'aaaaa', 'bbbbb', through 'eeeee'. Print only one pattern per line.

```
[for Ch := 'a' to 'e' do begin
   for i := 1 to 5 do write (Ch);
   writeln
end;]
```

39 • Write a program that prints every possible 5-letter combination of the letters 'a' through 'e'.

```
[for Ch1 := 'a' to 'e' do
   for Ch2 := 'a' to 'e' do
      for Ch3 := 'a' to 'e' do
         for Ch4 := 'a' to 'e' do
            for Ch5 := 'a' to 'e' do
               writeln (Ch1, Ch2, Ch3, Ch4, Ch5);]
```

40 • Write a program that sums the first 50 terms of the series:

```
1/2 + 1/3 + 1/4 ...
1/2 + 2/3 + 3/4 ...
1/2 − 1/3 + 1/4 - ...
2/1 + 3/2 − 4/3 + ...
```

41 • Write a program that is given 10 lines of input, and prints only the first character from the first line, the second character from the second line, and so on.

42 • Write a program that is given 10 lines of input, and prints only the tenth character from the first line, the ninth character from the second line, and so on.

Chapter Five

Understanding code ...

1 • Which of these might be legal **case** constants?

false	−11	17
Time	´X´	chr(63)
3 + 1	Hour div 60	1..31

2 • Which of these are always legal **case** expressions? Sometimes? Never?

1	3*5	Time	HOUR	´D´
D	5.7	sqrt(4)	sqrt(Date)	1+9

3 • Simplify this **case** statement as much as possible:

```
case (Save mod 3) of
   2: writeln (´Tie´);
   0: writeln (´Losing´);
   1: writeln (´Tie´);
   3: writeln (´Winner´);
   4,5: writeln (´Demolish´)
end;
```

4 • Fix the bug: [**change type of Channel or case constants.**]

```
program TV (input, output);
   {Prints the network of channel 1 through 9.}
var Channel:  integer;
begin
   writeln (´Enter a channel from 1 through 9.´);
   readln (Channel);
   case Channel of
      ´1´,´3´,´6´,´8´:  writeln (´Suppressed networks.´);
      ´2´:  writeln (´CNN´);
      ´4´:  writeln (´NBC´);
      ´5´:  writeln (´ABC´);
      ´7´:  writeln (´CBS´);
      ´9´:  writeln (´Public Broadcasting System´)
   end
end.
```

5 • Fix the bug: [**needs compound statement.**]

```
case (Hour mod 4) of
   1: ;
   7: writeln (´Late.´);
   0, 2, 3, 4:  writeln (´On time´);
                writeln (´Performance.´)
end;
```

6 • What's the input? [3] Output is:

```
Heads I win
Tails you lose
5
Heads I win
```

```
readln (X);
for i := X to 6 do
   case i mod 3 of
      0:  writeln (´Heads I win´);
      1:  writeln (´Tails you lose´);
      2:  writeln (i)
   end;
```

7 • Is this a legal **case** statement? If not, why not?

```
case Vowel of
  ´a´: ;
  ´e´: ;
  ´i´: ;
  ´o´: ;
  ´u´: ;
end;
```

8 • What's the output? [**2** \<cr\> **Heads I win** \<cr\> **Tails you lose** \<cr\> **2**]

```
for i := 2 to 5 do
  case i mod 3 of
    0: writeln (´Heads I win ´);
    1: writeln (´Tails you lose ´);
    2: writeln (i)
  end;
```

9 • Where's the bug? [**missing h**]

```
{Count letters a through d and e through i}
LowCount := 0;
HighCount := 0;
for Ch := ´a´ to ´i´ do
  case Ch of
    ´a´,´b´,´c´,´d´: LowCount := LowCount + 1;
    ´e´,´f´,´g´,´i´: HighCount := HighCount + 1
  end;
```

10 • Where's the bug? [**Extra read(Ch) at end of case statement.**]

```
{Print only the letters 'a' and 'd' in an input sequence. Input may be 'a' through 'e'.)
for i := 1 to 50 do begin
  read (Ch);
  case Ch of
    ´a´,´d´: write (Ch);
    ´b´,´c´,´e´: read (Ch)
  end
end;
writeln;
```

11 • Simplify this code segment.

```
[for i := 1 to 50 do begin
  read (Ch);
  writeln (Ch, Ch)
end;]
```

```
{Doubles each input character. Input is limited to ´a´ through ´d´}
for i := 1 to 50 do begin
  read (Ch);
  case Ch of
    ´a´: writeln (´aa ´);
    ´b´: writeln (´bb ´);
    ´c´: writeln (´cc ´);
    ´d´: writeln (´dd ´);
  end
end;
```

12 • What's the output? Assume that procedure *Print* is:

```
procedure Print (LetterNumber: integer);
  begin
    case LetterNumber of
      1: write ('w');
      2: write ('h');
      3,5: write ('e');
      4: write ('r');
      6: write ('a');
      7: write ('s')
    end;
  end; {Print}
```

[whereas wherea where wher whe wh w]

```
First := 1;
for Last := 7 downto First do begin
  for LetterNumber := First to Last do
    Print (LetterNumber);
  write ('  ')
end;
writeln;
```

13 • Assume procedure Print, above. What is the output of this program segment?

[w
wh h
whe he e
wher her er r
where here ere re e
wherea herea erea rea ea a
whereas hereas ereas reas eas as s]

```
for Outer := 1 to 7 do begin
  for Middle := 1 to Outer do begin
    for Inner := Middle to Outer do
      Print (Inner);
    write ('  ')
  end;
  writeln
end;
```

14 • Find the bug. **[Increments the wrong counts.]**

```
{Count the number of positive digits, negative digits, and zeros in 50 input numbers.}
PosCount := 0; NegCount := 0; ZeroCount := 0;
for i := 1 to 50 do begin
  read (Number);  {Assume Number is always a one-digit integer.}
  case Number of
    -9,-8,-7,-6,-5,-4,-3,-2,-1: PosCount := PosCount + 1;
    9,8,7,6,5,4,3,2,1: NegCount := NegCount + 1;
    0: ZeroCount := ZeroCount + 1
  end
end;
writeln (PosCount, NegCount, ZeroCount);
```

15 • Find the bug. [**Sets counters to zero each time through.**]

```
program CapitalCount (input, output);
   {Counts capital and lower case letters.  Assume input is
   in range 'a' through 'd' and 'A' through 'D'.}
var Letter: char;
Caps, Lower, i, Limit: integer;
begin
   writeln ('How many input characters will there be?')'
   readln (Limit);
   for i := 1 to Limit do begin
      Caps := 0;
      Lower := 0;
      read (Letter);
      case Letter of
         'a','b','c','d': Lower := Lower + 1;
         'A','B','C','D': Caps := Caps + 1
      end
   end;
   writeln ('Number of caps was ', Caps, '.  Number of lower-case was ', Lower)
end.
```

16 • What's the output? [**ab*cdaadhg?gh**] Here's the input: abeecdaadhgffgh

```
for i := 1 to 11 do begin
   read (Ch);
   case Ch of
      'a','b','c','d': write (Ch);
      'e': begin
             read (Ch);
             case Ch of
                'e': write ('*');
                'f','g','h': write ('e', Ch)
             end
           end;
      'f': begin
             read (Ch);
             case Ch of
                'f': write ('?');
                'e','g','h': write ('f', Ch)
             end
           end;
      'g': begin
             read (Ch);
             case Ch of
                'g': write ('!');
                'e','f','h': write ('g', Ch)
             end
           end;
      'h': begin
             read (Ch);
             case Ch of
                'h': write ('$');
                'e','f','g': write ('h', Ch)
             end;
           end
   end
end;
writeln;
```

17 • Here's the output: a?baba*a   What was the input? [**bacacbca**]

```
for i := 1 to 6 do begin
   read (Ch);
   case Ch of
      'a': write (Ch);
      'b': begin
              write ('a');
              read (Ch);
              case Ch of
                 'a': write ('?');
                 'b': write ('\*');
                 'c': write ('*')
              end
           end;
      'c': write ('b')
   end
end;
writeln;
```

Short responses ...

18 • What is a case expression? A case constant? Give examples.

19 • A Pascal system is supposed to detect an error if the value of the case expression is not represented in the case constant list. Write a program that will test your system, and lets you know if it correctly detects the error.

20 • What types may the case expression and case constants be? Are any types forbidden?

21 • What is a brute force solution? How is it different from an elegant solution? Give an example of each.

22 • What are three reasons you might use a brute force solution even if you suspect that a more elegant solution exists?

23 • It has been said that although program testing may show the presence of bugs, it can't guarantee their absence. What does this mean? Describe the difference between testing and debugging.

24 • What is a stub program? Use pictures to describe a stub program, if necessary.

25 • Would you say that stub programming is a top-down or bottom-up programming technique? Why?

26 • What is a stub procedure (or dummy procedure)? Why is it useful? When should it be used? Give an example.

27 • In reading through your roommate's Computer Science homework, you come across this segment of code:

```
procedure HardStuff (Data: integer;  var Results: char);
begin
   Results := 'A';
   writeln ('In procedure HardStuff.  Data and Results are', Data, Results)
end;
```

What is the purpose of this procedure? What is your roommate up to?

28 • What is Big O notation? How is it useful?

29 • In discussing an algorithm's efficiency, we mentioned the use of 'proportional measures' of program running time. What does it mean to say that a particular algorithm runs in time proportional to N? What is N?

30 • What is the difference between algorithms with linear running time, and those with constant running time? Give examples.

Write a program that ...

31 • Write a program that reads 100 input characters, and counts every i that is followed by an e, o, or u. Assume that input consists only of the vowels a, e, i, o, and u.

32 • Write a program that reads 100 input characters, and counts punctuation and digit characters. Input consists only of these characters and the space character.

33 • Write a program that acts as a calculator of sorts. It should add the twelve numbers following a +, subtract the nine numbers following a −, multiply the seven numbers following a *, and print the eight numbers following a : or ; . Assume that twenty of the symbols +, −, *, :, and ; will be supplied in all.

34 • Write a program that reads a total of 100 characters of input and follows these rules: It should ignore any character that is preceded by a 1, double (print twice) any character preceded by a +, triple any character preceded by a −, and echo all other characters. Assume that input consists only of the characters 1, +, −, and the letters a through e. Remember: there are exactly 100 input characters.

35 • Write a program that reads digit characters and counts the number of digits that are either 3, 5, or 6, and that are either 1, 4, or 9. Other digits should be ignored.

36 • Write a program that reads digit characters and counts the number of digits that are either 1, 2, or 3, and that are 3, 4, or 5.

37 • Write a program that reads a letter grade that consists of one of the capital letters A, B, C, D, or F, followed by a +, −, or space character. Print the value of the grade. Remember that an A+ is worth no more than an A, while an F− is worth no less than an F.

38 • Write a program that balances a checkbook. Its input begins with the *integer* number of transactions that are to follow, and a *real* starting balance. Each transaction (one per line) consists of an amount to credit or debit from the balance, preceded by a + or − sign. The program should end by printing the number and total value of credits, the number and total value of debits, the closing balance, and the difference between the starting and closing balances.

39 • Write a program that reads ten lines of input. Each line begins with a special character that has the following meaning:

> $ Find the total sums of, and average of, these lines.
> * Multiply these lines and print the final product.
> − Find the number of these lines, but ignore any values they include.

An *integer* value immediately follows the special character. Each line has only one *integer* value, besides the initial special character.

Chapter Six

Understanding code ...

1 • Suppose we have these variables, initialized as shown:

Alpha := true;   Ch := 'D';   Int := 3;   Beta := false;

What are the values of these expressions? Are there any type clashes or illegal expressions?

Beta	Alpha = Beta	Int <= 'B'
Ch > 'E'	Beta <> false	Ch <= 'D'
Beta <> Alpha	Ch <> Int	'A' < Ch < 'Z'

2 • Suppose that we have two boolean variables, initialized as shown:

Alpha := true;   Beta := false;

What is the value of each of these boolean expressions?

not Alpha and Beta	Alpha and not Beta	not (Alpha and Beta)
Alpha and Beta	Alpha or Beta	not (Alpha or Beta)
Beta or not Alpha	Alpha or not Beta	Beta or (Alpha and Beta)
(Alpha = Beta) or (Beta <> Alpha)		(Beta and Alpha) = false
true and (Alpha <> Beta)		

3 • Find the equivalent pairs of boolean expressions. [**Correct pairs are given—mix before using.**]

a)   First <> Last
b)   (First and not Last) or (Last and not First)
c)   First = Last
d)   (First and Last) or (not Last and not First)
e)   not First or not Last
f)   not (Last and First)
g)   not (Last or First)
h)   not First and not Last
i)   (First or Second) and Third
j)   (Third and First) or (Second and Third)
k)   (First and Second) or Third
l)   (Third or First) and (Second or Third)

4 • Write each of these as a boolean expression.

a)   I have more than enough money.
      [**Money > Enough**]
b)   A equals 6, but B neither equals A nor 7.
      [**(A = 6) and ((B<>A) and (B<>7))**]
c)   21 ≤ Date ≤ 27.
      [**(Date >= 21) and (Date <= 27)**]
d)   Age isn't between 20 and 30.
      [**not ((Age > 20) and (Age < 30)), (Age <= 20) or (Age >= 30)**]
e)   Ch equals '6' or 'T', while Count is less than 5.
      [**((Ch = '6') or (Ch = 'T')) and (Count < 5)**]
f)   Initial isn't a capital letter.
      [**(Initial< 'A') or (Initial> 'Z')), not (Initial in ['A'..'Z'])**]

5 • Are any of these assignments equivalent? Which ones? [**a−c, b−d−f**]

a)   Finished := Done;
b)   Finished := Done <> true;
c)   Finished := Done = true;
d)   Finished := Done = false;
e)   Finished := not Finished;
f)   Finished := not Done;

6 • Rewrite each sequence of statements as a single boolean assignment statement. Assume that all variables referred to have been initialized.

if Test > 5   [**Passed := Test > 5**]
  then Passed := true
  else Passed := false;

if Test = 6   [**Check := Test <> 6**]
  then if Test = 8
    then Check := true
    else Check := false
  else Check := true;

if Test = 7   [**Check := (Test <> 7) or ((Test = 7) and (Pass = 8))**]
  then if Pass = 8
    then Check := true
    else Check := false
  else Check := true;

if (First = 'A') or (Last = 'Z')   [**Answer := ((First='A') or (Last='Z')) and (Second='B')**]
  then if Second = 'B'
    then Answer := true
    else Answer := false
  else Answer := false;

if (First = 'A') or (Last = 'Z')   [**Answer := (((First='A') or (Last='Z')) and (Second='B'))**
  then if Second = 'B'   **or ((First<>'A') and (Last<>'Z'))**]
    then Answer := true
    else Answer := false
  else Answer := true;

7 • Rewrite the following as a single **if** statement. Simplify the assignment as much as possible.

[**if Time >= 5 then Time := 2 * Time**]

if Time >= 5 then Time := Time * 4;
if Time >= 20 then Time := Time div 2;

8 • Rewrite this as a single **if** statement. Simplify the assignment as much as possible.

[**if Age > 9 then Age := 3 + Age**]

if Age > 9 then Age := 7 + 3 * Age;
if Age > 36 then Age := 5 − Age div 3;

9 • Rewrite this as an **if** statement with an **else** part, rather than as two **if** statements.

[**if Time < 37 then Time := Time div 4 else Time := 3 * Time**]

if Time < 37 then Time := Time div 4;
if Time > 36 then Time := 3 * Time;

10 • Rewrite this as a sequence of two **if** statements, rather than as a single **if** statement with an **else** part. Assume that procedure *DoSomethingTo* will modify *Day*.

[**if Day >= 3 then writeln ('Today''s the day.')**
if Day < 3 then DoSomethingTo (Day)]

if Day < 3
  then DoSomethingTo (Day)
  else writeln ('Today''s the day.');

11 • Rewrite this as a single **if** statement with an **else** part, rather than as the nested statement shown below. Assume that all variables have been initialized.

[**if (Number > 4) and Correct then writeln ('A Ok.') else writeln ('Not today.')**]

```
if Number > 4
   then begin
      if Correct then writeln ('A Ok.')
                 else writeln ('Not today.')
   end
   else writeln ('Not today.');
```

12 • Can this be written as a single **if** statement with an **else** part? Do it if you can.

[**if (A >= 3) and (B < 6) then writeln ('Hi there.') else writeln ('Bye now.')**]

```
if (A >= 3) and (B < 6) then
   writeln ('Hi there.')
if (6 <= B) or (2 >= A) then
   writeln ('Bye now.')
```

13 • What is the output of this program? [**Great Stuff**]

```
program Stereo (input, output);
var Radio, TurnTable, Cassette, Tape: boolean;
begin
   Radio := true;
   TurnTable := not Radio;
   Cassette := TurnTable or Radio;
   Tape := not Cassette;
   if Radio and not Tape
      then if Tape and Cassette
         then writeln ('Good Stuff')
         else writeln ('Great Stuff')
      else writeln ('Fantastic Stuff')
end.
```

14 • Find the bug: [**>= should be >**]

```
{Counts numbers greater than 6}
Count := 0;
for i := 1 to 10 do begin
  read (Number);
  if Number >= 6 then
    Count := Count + 1
end;
```

15 • Find the bug: [**and should be or**]

```
{Counts numbers outside range −5 through 5}
Count := 0;
for i := 1 to 50 do begin
  read (Number);
  if (Number >= 5) and (Number <= −5) then
    Count := Count + 1
end;
```

16 • Find the bug. [**or should be and**]

```
{Count positive even numbers.}
Count := 0;
for i := 50 do begin
  read (Number);
  if (Number > 0) or (not odd(Number)) then
    Count := Count + 1
end;
```

17 • Find the bug. [**or should be and**]

```
{Count characters that are not 'T' or '5'}
Count := 0;
for i := 1 to 50 do begin
    read (Ch);
    if (Ch <> 'T') or (Ch <> '5') then
        Count := Count + 1
end;
writeln (Count, ' characters were not T or 5.');
```

18 • Here's the input: 1 4 3 6 8 0 5 2 9 0 1 5 8 0 3   What's the output? [**toggles between printing odds and evens, starting with odds and flipping at zeros: 1 3 2 1 5**]

```
tog := 0;
for i := 1 to 15 do begin
    read (N);
    if N = 0
        then tog := tog + 1
        else if odd (N + tog)
            then write (N)
end;
writeln;
```

19 • Here's the output: 1 −4 3 −6 −8 −5 2 −9 1 5 −8 −3   What was the input? [**toggles between echoing as positive or negative, starting with odds positive, evens negative, and flipping at zero. Input is: 1 4 3 6 8 0 5 2 9 0 1 5 8 0 3**]

```
tog := 0;
for i := 1 to 15 do begin
    read (N);
    if N = 0
        then tog := tog + 1
        else if odd (N + tog)
            then write (N)
            else write (−N)
end;
writeln;
```

20 • Here's the output: 15 12 20 10 64 36 18 24 21   What's the input? [**3 12 1 10 2 8 1 18 3 21**] [easier if '1 18' is changed to '1 19']

```
for i := 1 to 5 do begin
    read (N, M);
    if N = 1 then write (2*M)
            else if N = 2 then write (M*M)
                        else if N = 3 then write (M+3)
end;
if odd (N) then write (M);
writeln;
```

21 • The output is shown below. What's the input? [**10 8 9**]

```
20  18  20
18  16  16
19  17  18
```

```
for i := 1 to 3 do begin
   read (N);
   A := N = 6;
   B := odd (N);
   C := not (A or B);
   if B and C then write (N * N)
               else write (N + 10);
   if A and C then write (3 * N)
               else write (N + 8);
   if A and B then write (N − 2)
               else write (2 * N)
end;
```

22 • What's the output? The input is: AEBCBCCDCEDDFDEDAAEB [E 1 (counts 1 A, 2 B's, 3 C's, etc.)]

```
A := 'A';
B := 0;
for i := 1 to 20 do begin
   read (C);
   if C = A then begin
               B := B + 1;
               if B = 1 + (ord (C) − ord ('A') then begin
                                          B := 0;
                                          A := succ(A)
                              end
                 end
end;
writeln (A, B);
```

23 • What's the input? The output is: 19 14 4 1 7 2 9 7 11 3 16 10 12 4 6 3 5 0 20 10 [**19 5 3 4 5 7 9 2 11 8 16 6 8 12 3 6 5 5 20 10**]

```
for i := 1 to 10 do begin
   read (F,S);
   if (F−S)>0 then write (F, F−S)
               else write (S, S−F)
end;
writeln;
```

24 • What's the output? The input (exactly 60 characters long) is:

My deed was predicated on editing the information he posted.

[2 (counts 'ed ' endings)]

```
Count := 0;
read (Ch);
for i := 1 to 30 do
   if Ch = 'e'
      then begin
         read (Ch);
         if Ch = 'd' then begin
            read (Ch);
            if Ch = ' ' then Count := Count + 1
         end
      end
      else read (Ch);
writeln (Count);
```

Short responses ...

25 • What is the difference between the relational operators and the *boolean* operators?

26 • What are the values a *boolean* variable may represent? Give three example expressions for each of the possibble *boolean* values.

27 • When **if** statements are nested, what determines which statement an **else** part belongs to? Is

there any way to change this association? Give an example.

28 • Suppose that you didn't know Pascal's rule for associating nested **if** statements with the appropriate **else** parts. Write a sample program, or programs, that would let you know which **if** statement a subsequent **else** belonged to.

29 • Why must relational expressions always be put in parentheses when they appear as part of a longer *boolean* expression?

30 • What bugs do these statements contain? Why? How would you fix them?

```
if not Ch in ['A'..'Z'] then
    writeln ('Not a capital letter ');

if Ch >= 'A' and Ch <= 'Z' then
    writeln ('It is a capital letter ');

if Ch not 'A' or 'Z' then
    writeln ('Neither A nor Z. ');
```

31 • Is there anything unusual or unnecessary about this statement? What? Why? How would you change it?

```
if (Testing = true) or (Failed = false) then
    Continue;
```

32 • What does it mean to say that a program is robust?

33 • What does it mean to say that *boolean* expressions are fully evaluated? Give an example.

34 • What is the bug in this program segment? It's supposed to add the odd numbers between Low and High, inclusive. Will the program compile? Will it run?

```
Sum := 0;
for Count := Low to High do begin
    writeln (Count);
    if odd (Count) then;
        Sum := Sum + Count
end;
```

35 • What is embedded debugging code? Why is it used? Give an example.

36 • In the text we discussed the idea of embedding code to help with debugging. We suggested using a constant (like *DEBUGGING*) whose value would set the proper level of detail for program diagnostics.
Show how code for debugging might be embedded in a program. Distinguish between three uses of a *DEBUGGING* variable:

1.   as a *boolean* -valued variable.
2.   as an *integer* variable used with a **case** statement.
3.   as an *integer* variable used with nested **if** statements to create additive debugging levels.

37 • Is there any difference between these program segments? What is it? Under what circumstances might they be equivalent? Discuss.

```
read (Date);    {first segment}
if Date < 0 then
    DealWith (Date, 0);
if (Date >= 0) and (Date < 5) then
    DealWith (Date, 5);
if (Date >= 5) and (Date < 10) then
    DealWith (Date, 10);

read (Date);    {second segment}
if Date < 0
    then DealWith (Date, 0)
    else if Date < 5
        then DealWith (Date, 5)
        else if Date < 10
            then DealWith (Date, 10);
```

Write a program that ...

38 • Write a program that finds the smallest even number, largest odd number, and their positions in a sequence of 50 input *integers* .

39 • Write a program that looks though 50 input characters and counts the number of T's, the number of E's that are followed by F's, and the number of G's that are preceded by H's.

40 • Write a program that counts the number of 'ing' endings in an input sample of 100 characters.

41 • Write a program that finds the second largest of 20 input numbers.

42 • Write a program that prints the odd Fibonacci numbers among the first 20 in the sequence, starting 1, 1, 2 ....

43 • Write a program that reads four characters, then prints them in descending order. Assume that you have a procedure that can order two characters.

44 • Write a program that reads 100 input numbers, averages the positive and negative numbers seperately, and prints the averages.

45 • Imagine that 100 *integer* values are labeled by position: 1, 2, 3, etc. Write a program that reads the 100 *integers* , and keeps track of how many of them have the same value as their position. For example, in the sequence: 1 5 3 4 2, exactly three numbers (1, 3, 4) have the same value as their positions.

46 • Write a program that reads 100 input characters. It should look for the first 'A', then look for the first 2 'B's, then the first 3 C's, and so on. Finish by printing the letter the program is currently looking for, and the count of that letter seen so far.

47 • Write a program that reads 100 input *integers* , and keeps track of those that are even, even and divisible by 3, odd, and odd and divisible by 7.

48 • Write a program that reads 100 characters. Keep a running total of the distance from the letter 'A' of each capital letter, of the distance from the letter 'z' for each lower-case letter, and of the total number of non-letters.

49 • Write a program that reads 100 input *integers* , and finds the largest and smallest differences between two succeeding numbers. For instance, if input is: 1 10 17 25 23, the largest difference is 9 (10−1), and the smallest difference is 2 (25−23).

50 • Write a function that returns *true* if:

> its argument is [in the range 15..35] [a vowel] [not a vowel]
> [not a puncutation mark] [is a number evenly divisible by both 23 and 17]
> [has 4 digits] [is a perfect square] [there is an even remainder when the
> first argument divides the second argument] [the first argument (a character)
> is in the ordinal position given by the second argument] [its two *char*
> arguments are both upper-case, lower-case, or digits]

Chapter Seven

Understanding code ...

1 • Which of these pairs of code segments are identical? [**second and third pair**]

```
i := 5;                          i := 5;
repeat                           while i > = 5 do
   i := i − 1                       i := i − 1;
until i < 1;
```

```
while i > 5 do                   if i > 5 then
   i := i div 2;                    repeat
                                 i := i div 2
                                    until i < = 5;
```

```
sum := 0;                        sum := 0;
begin                            read (n);
   read (n);                     repeat
   repeat                           begin
      sum := sum + n;                  sum := sum + n;
      read (n)                         read (n)
   until n = 5                      end
end;                             until n = 5;
```

```
Foo := true;                     repeat
while (Foo and Bar) do begin        read (Ch1, Ch2);
   read (Ch1, Ch2);                 Foo := Ch1 = Ch2;
   Foo := Ch1 = Ch2;                Bar := Ch2 = ´X´
   Bar := Ch2 = ´X´             until not Foo or not Bar;
end;
```

NOTE: The next series of questions are given in schematic form. They are easily made more difficult by expanding the 'action' to something like:

```
read (Num1, Num2);
A := odd (Num1);
B := Num2 > = Num1;   etc.
```

2 • Which of these are equivalent code segments? [**a, b**]

```
a)      repeat
            action
        until not A or not B;
```

```
b)      action;
        while A and B do
            action;
```

```
c)      action;
        while A or B do
            action;
```

3 • Rewrite this code segment using a **while** loop, and no **if** or **repeat**: [**while not A or B do action**]

```
if not A or B then
   repeat
      action
   until A and not B;
```

4 • Rewrite this code segment using a **while** loop, with no **if** or **repeat**: [**action; while A or B do action**]

```
repeat
   action
until not (A or B);
```

5 • Rewrite this code segment using other control statements. Do not use a **while** loop.

> [**if A and not B then**
>   **repeat**
>   **action**
>   **until not A or B**]

    while A and not B do
      action;

6 • Rewrite this code segment using other control statements. Do not use a **while** loop.

> [**if A or B then**
>   **repeat**
>   **action**
>   **until not (A or B)**]

    while A or B do
      action;

7 • Rewrite this code segment without using a **while** statement: [**repeat action until (A or B) and C**]

    action;
    while (not A and not B) or not C do
      action;

8 • Rewrite this code segment without using a **repeat** statement: [**action; while (A and B) or C do action**]

    repeat
      action
    until not (A or B) and not C;

9 • Rewrite this segment without using a **while** statement:

> [**repeat**
>   **read (Ch);**
>   **if Ch = '#' then readln;**
>   **write (Ch)**
> **until Ch = '?';**]

    read (Ch);
    if Ch = '#' then readln;
    write (Ch);
    while Ch <> '?' do begin
      read (Ch);
      if Ch = '#' then readln;
      write (Ch)
    end;

10 • Rewrite this segment using a **repeat** statement, rather than a **while**.

> [**repeat**
>   **read (Ch);**
>   **write (Ch)**
> **until Ch = '#';**]

    read (Ch);
    write (Ch);
    while Ch <> '#' do begin
      read (Ch);
      write (Ch)
    end;

11 • Rewrite this program segment using a **while** loop. Simplify if possible, but preserve the segment's effect.

    [i : = 20; read (Ch); while Ch < > ´a´ do read (Ch);]

```
i := 20;
repeat
   read (Ch);
   Done := (Ch = ´a´) or (i < 10)
until Done;
```

12 • Rewrite this segment using a **for** loop, rather than a **while**. Simplify if possible, but preserve the segment's effect.

    [for i : = 1 to 9 do read (Ch); i : = 10; j : = 12;]

```
i := 1;
j := 12;
while (i < 10) and (j > 11) do begin
   read (Ch);
   i := i + 1
end;
```

13 • Here's the input, what's the output? [**EL PASO is hot, just HOT, mcGRAW said.** (Prints remainder of word in caps following a cap.)]

    El Paso is hot, just HOT, mcGraw said.

```
repeat
   read (Ch);
   if Ch in [´A´..´Z´] then
      repeat
        write (Ch);
        read (Ch);
        if Ch in [´a´..´z´] then
           Ch := chr(ord(Ch) + ord(´A´) − ord(´a´))
      until (Ch = ´ ´) or (Ch = ´.´);
   write (Ch)
until Ch = ´.´;
writeln;
```

14 • Here's the input, what's the output? [**suppress output of any word beginning with a cap**]

    Something is noThing When programs Work.

```
repeat
   read (Ch);
   if Ch in [´A´..´Z´]
      then repeat
              read (Ch)
           until (Ch = ´ ´) or (Ch = ´.´)
      else repeat
              write (Ch);
              read (Ch)
           until (Ch = ´ ´) or (Ch = ´.´);
   write (Ch)
until Ch = ´.´;
writeln;
```

58   Teaching Introductory Programming

15 • Here's the input, what's the output? [−6 −31 2 −5 8 −1 −1]

    7 32 −3 6 −9 0 5 7

```
NewCount := 0;
repeat
  read (Number);
  if (Number > 0) and (Number < > 5) then begin
    NewNumber := 0 − Number;
    NewNumber := NewNumber + 1
  end;
  NewCount := NewCount + 1;
  if Number < = 0 then begin
    NewNumber := Number + 1;
    NewNumber := 0 − NewNumber
  end;
  write (NewNumber)
until (Number = 5) or (NewCount > 6);
writeln;
```

16 • Here's the output: 7 20 7 15 23 9 5 8 8 8 What's the input? [20 7 7 15 9 23 5 8 8 8]

```
repeat
  read (Number1, Number2);
  if abs (Number1 − Number2) > 10
    then writeln (Number2, Number1)
    else writeln (Number1, Number2)
until (Number1 − Number2) = 0;
```

17 • Here's the input: 83852   What's the output? [26 5]

```
readln (Number);
C := 10;
B := 0;
A := 0;
repeat
  B := B + 1;
  Digit := Number mod C;
  A := A + Digit div (C div 10);
  Number := Number − Digit;
  C := C * 10
until Number = 0;
writeln (A, B);
```

18 • Here's the output: 10 −73 22 3 41 18 14 −20   What was the input? [10 83 22 19 41 23 14 34]

```
repeat
  read (First, Second);
  write (First, First − Second)
until abs (First − Second) = 20;
writeln;
```

19 • This segment of code is supposed to read numbers, and negate and echo any number that is preceded by a 5, 7, or 9. The value 777 marks the end of valid input. Is it possible for program output to include the value −777? The value −5? Will the sentinel ever be printed? [**yes, yes, only if the sentinal is preceded by 5, 7, or 9**]

```
read (Number);
while Number <> 777 do begin
   if Number in [5,7,9] then begin
       read (Number);
       Number := 0 − Number
   end;
   writeln (Number);
   if Number <> 777 then
       read (Number)
end;
```

20 • Here's the input, what's the output? [**prints only evens, then only odds, etc. Toggle is zero, negative ends input.**]

17 43 18 9 6 0 21 99 43 0 65 22 88 94 0 16 17 18 19 −6

```
program Toggle (input,output);
var Number, Tog: integer;
begin
   Tog := 1;
   read(Number);
   while Number >= 0 do begin
     if odd (Number + Tog) and (Number <> 0) then write (Number);
     if (Number = 0) and (Tog = 1)
        then Tog := 0
        else if (Number = 0) and (Tog = 0)
           then Tog := Tog + 1;
     read (Number)
   end;
   writeln
end.
```

21 • Here's the output, what's the input? [**changes sign of input until reading 7, then leaves it alone until reading 5. Ends with 0.**]

5 −9 6 −4 −3 7 −7 −5 −9 6 −4 −3 7 −5 5 5 0

```
program Mystery (input,output);
var A,B: integer;
begin
   B := −1;
   read (A);
   while A <> 0 do begin
      if A = 7 then B := 1;
      if A = 5 then B := −1;
      write (A * B);
      read (A)
   end;
   writeln
end.
```

Short responses ...

22 • What is the difference between a **repeat** loop and a **while** loop?

23 • What is an entry condition? An exit condition? Give examples.

24 • The following loop contains a bug. What is it? Why? [**doesn't set exit condition**]

```
while Checking and not Finished do begin
    read (Choice);
    if not Finished and (Choice = 'Q') then
        writeln ('Still Playing');
    readln (Value);
    if Checking then
        Value := 2 * Value
end;
```

25 • What is program robustness? Give an example of a feature that makes a program robust.

26 • What is a sentinel? What are sentinels used for?

27 • What does it mean to say that a program should degrade gracefully? Describe an example of graceful program degradation.

28 • What is an execution profile of a program? How is it useful?

29 • The text refers to a loop's *boundary conditions*, and suggests that they should be checked especially carefully. What does this mean? What are a loop's boundary conditions?

30 • What is an off-by-one error? Can you give an example of this kind of error?

31 • The following program segment expects a series of *integer* values as input. After it reads a 'command' number, the program is supposed to echo the number, then ignore that many input values. For instance, if it reads a 3 as the 'command', the program is supposed to print a 3 and ignore the next 3 numbers. If the 'command' is a negative number, the program should end. Will the program segment work as desired? Explain. Rewrite the segment if necessary. [**program will stop if one of the 'ignored' numbers is negative.**]

```
read (Number);
while Number >= 0 do begin
    writeln (Number);
    for i := 1 to Number do
        if Number >= 0 then read (Number);
    if Number >= 0 then read (Number)
end;
```

Write a program that ...

32 • Write a program that finds the third time the letter 'F' appears in input, and prints its position.

33 • Write a program that adds the positive numbers in a sequence of input values that terminates with zero. Your program should announce if there are no positive numbers at all.

34 • Write a program that reads a sequence of *integers* that ends with zero. It should keep track of positive and negative input separately, and print the average of each.

35 • Write a program that counts and prints the number of times the letter 'T' is followed by the letter 'S.' Your program should stop when it reads a '7', or finds eleven T's (whether or not each is followed by an 'S'), or reads fifty characters in all.

36 • Write a program that finds the lowest value N for which N factorial exceeds N to the fourth power.

37 • Write a program that reads a sequence of input *integers*, and prints the largest value, the smallest value, and their positions in the sequence. The sequence ends with the value 7, which is not part of the sequence.

38 • Write a program that reads a sequence of *integers*, and prints every number whose position equals the number itself. The sequence begins with the first number (of course), and ends with either a zero, or a number that is evenly divisible by 987.

39 • Suppose that you have a can of whipped cream. Every second the nozzle is held open, 2% of the whipped cream remaining in the can will spurt out. How many seconds will it take to empty half the can?

40 • Write a program that prints the difference of successive input values until the difference between them exceeds 15. The program should also end immediately if the value 3, or any negative number, is read.

41 • Write a program that counts the number of vowels (a, e, i, o, and u) in a sequence of input characters. Spotting the end of input will be hard. Either the last legal input value will *be a 'u' or a*

'z' will *follow* the last legal input value.

42 • Write a program that reads *char* values. Whenever a 'z' is read, it should begin to echo the characters it reads, and whenever an 'a' is read it should *not* echo subsequent characters. The letter 'm' follows the last legal input character. Assume that the first input character will be a 'z'.

Chapter Eight

Understanding code ...

1 • Which of these is equivalent to the call *readln*? [**f**]

    a)   while not eof do read (Ch); write (Ch);
    b)   while not eoln do read (Ch); write (Ch);
    c)   while not eof do readln;
    d)   while not eof do read (Ch); read (Ch);
    e)   while not eoln do read (Ch);
    f)   while not eoln do read (Ch); read (Ch);
    g)   while not eoln do readln;
    h)   can't be done.

2 • Suppose that a program has several lines of input available. Which of these discards all but the last line; i.e. leaves you about to read the last line of input? [**d**]

    a)   while not eof do readln;
    b)   while not (eof −1) do readln;
    c)   while not eoln do readln;
    d)   can't be done.

3 • Which are the equivalent pairs? [**given in order; mix before using.**]

    a)   while not eoln do read (Ch); writeln; read (Ch);
    b)   readln; writeln; Ch := ' ';
    c)   while not eof do read (Ch);
    d)   while not eof do readln; Ch := ' ';
    e)   while not eoln do readln;
    f)   can't be matched.

4 • Which of these code segments are equivalent? [**a−c, b−d**]

```
a) while not eof do begin          b) while not eof do begin
     while not eoln do begin            while not eoln do begin
       read (Ch);                          write (Ch);
       write (Ch)                          read (Ch)
     end;                               end;
     readln;                            readln;
     writeln                            writeln
   end;                               end;


c) while not eof do begin          d) while not eof do begin
     while not eoln do begin            while not eoln do begin
       read (Ch);                          write (Ch);
       write (Ch)                          read (Ch)
     end;                               end;
     writeln;                           writeln;
     readln                             readln
   end;                               end;
```

5 • Which pair is equivalent? [**b−c**]

```
a) while not eoln do begin          b) while not eoln do begin
     read (Ch);                           if not eoln then read (Ch);
     if not eoln then read (Ch);          read (Ch);
     write (Ch)                           write (Ch)
   end;                                 end;


c) while not eoln do begin
     read (Ch);
     read (Ch);
     write (Ch)
   end;
```

NOTE: The next series of questions is supplied as a sequence of completed programs. They are suitable for use as 'here's the input, what's the output?', 'here's the output, what's the input?', 'what does this (uncommented) program do?', 'write a program that ...', etc.

6 • Good for 'what's the output?', with bad identifiers and unlabeled output.

```pascal
program NumberOfChars (input, output);
{Counts the number of lines, chars per line, and average chars/line.}
var NumberOfLines, Sum, NumberOfChars: integer;
    Ch: char;
begin
  NumberOfLines := 0;
  Sum := 0;
  while not eof do begin
    NumberOfLines := NumberOfLines + 1;
    NumberOfChars := 0;
    while not eoln do begin
      read(Ch);
      NumberOfChars := NumberOfChars + 1
    end;
    writeln ('Number of chars was ', NumberOfChars);
    Sum := Sum + NumberOfChars;
    readln
  end;
  writeln ('The average was ', Sum div NumberOfLines);
  writeln(' Total number of lines was ', NumberOfLines)
end.
```

7 • 'What does this do?', 'what's the output?', 'write a program ...', or introduce a bug, esp. an initialization bug.

```pascal
program DollarAmounts (input, output);
{Assume that each '$' is followed by a real dollar amount. Program prints value
of lines with smallest and largest average amounts, and average of all figures.}
var TotalCount, LineCount: integer;
    TotalSum, LineSum, Dollar, Biggest, Smallest: real;
    Ch: char;
begin
  Biggest := -MAXINT;
  Smallest := MAXINT;
  TotalSum := 0;
  TotalCount := 0;
  while not eof do begin
    LineCount := 0;
    LineSum := 0;
    while not eoln do begin
      read(Ch);
      if Ch = '$' then begin
        read(Dollar);
        LineSum := LineSum + Dollar;
        LineCount := LineCount + 1
      end
    end;
    if LineSum/LineCount > Biggest then Biggest := LineSum;
    if LineSum/LineCount < Smallest then Smallest := LineSum;
    TotalCount := TotalCount + LineCount;
    TotalSum := TotalSum + LineSum;
    readln
  end;
  write(' The line with the largest average totaled ', Biggest);
  writeln(' The line with the smallest average totaled ', Smallest);
  writeln(' The average dollar entry was ', TotalSum/TotalCount)
end.
```

8 • 'What does this program do?' or 'write a program ...'

```
program LineLength (input, output);
{Echos text while finding the longest, shortest, and average line length.}
var Longest, Shortest, NumberOfLines, LengthSum, Length: integer;
    Ch: char;
begin
   Longest := -MAXINT;
   Shortest := MAXINT;
   NumberOfLines := 0;
   LengthSum := 0;
   while not eof do begin
      NumberOfLines := NumberOfLines + 1;
      Length := 0;
      while not eoln do begin
         read (Ch);
         write (Ch);
         Length := Length + 1
      end;
      if Length < Shortest then Shortest := Length;
      if Length > Longest then Longest := Length;
      LengthSum := LengthSum + Length;
      readln;
      writeln
   end;
   writeln ('The longest line was ', Longest);
   writeln ('The shortest line was ', Shortest);
   writeln ('The average length was ', LengthSum div NumberOfLines)
end.
```

9 • 'What's the output?' or 'write a program ...'.

```
program Exclaim (input, output);
{Reads and echos text, preserving line structure. In addition, the first
'!' precedes a target character. Program reports the number of times the
target character appears.}
var Count: integer;
    Target, Ch: char;
    Found: boolean;
begin
   Count := 0;
   Found := false;
   while not eof do begin
      while not eoln do begin
         read (Ch);
         if (Ch = '!') and not Found then begin
            read (Target);
            write (Ch, Target);
            Found := true;
            Count := 1
         end
         else begin
            if Found and (Ch = Target) then Count := Count + 1;
            write (Ch)
         end
      end;
      writeln;
      readln
   end;
   writeln ('The number of targets was ', Count)
end.
```

65

10 • 'What's the input/output?', 'what does it do?', or 'write a program ...'

```
program FindOne (input,output);
{Finds empty input lines.}
begin
   while not eof do begin
      if eoln then
         writeln ('Found it! ');
      readln
   end
end.
```

11 • 'What's the input/output?', 'what does it do?', or 'write a program ...'

```
program FindTwo (input,output);
{Finds pairs of empty input lines.}
begin
   while not eof do begin
      if eoln then begin
         readln;
         if eoln then writeln ('Found it! ')
      end;
      readln
   end
end.
```

12 • 'What's the input/output?', 'what does it do?', or 'write a program ...'

```
program BlankLine (input, output);
{Echos input, getting rid of all empty lines, but printing a count
of how many consecutive empty lines there were.}
var Count: integer;
    Ch: char;
    Finished: boolean;
begin
   repeat
      Count := 0;
      Finished := false;
      while not eof and not Finished do
         if eoln do begin
            readln;
            Count := Count + 1
         end
         else Finished := true;
      if Count > 0 then writeln (Count);
      if not eof then begin
         while not eoln do begin
            read (Ch);
            write (Ch)
         end;
         readln;
         writeln
      end
   until eof
end.
```

13 • 'What's the input?', 'what does it do?'

```
program LastChar (input, output);
{Reads and echos text, preserving line structure.  In addition, every character
is preceded by the final character of the previous line (assume blank for first line.}
var Ch, LastCh: char;
begin
    LastCh := ' ';
    while not eof do begin
        while not eoln do begin
            write (LastCh);
            read (Ch);
            write (Ch)
        end;
        LastCh := Ch;
        readln;
        writeln
    end
end.
```

14 • 'Here's the input/output', 'write a program ...'

```
program MatchLetter (input, output);
{Reads and echos text.  In addition, looks for, and prints count of,
lines starting with last letter of previous line (assume blank at start).
Blank input lines do not change 'last' letter.}
var Ch, Target:  char;
    Special:  integer;
begin
    Special := 0;
    Target := ' ';
    while not eof do begin
        if eoln
            then writeln  {note that Target is not updated on blank input lines.}
            else begin
                read (Ch);
                if Ch = Target then Special := Special + 1;
                while not eoln do begin
                    write (Ch);
                    read (Ch)
                end;
                Target := Ch;
                writeln (Ch);
            end; {if not eoln}
        readln
    end; {not eof}
    writeln (Special)
end.
```

15 • 'What's the input/output?', 'write a program ...'

```
program MixUp (input, output);
{Reads and echos text.  In addition, prints every M as a <CR>, every <CR> as
an x, and every x as an M.}
var Ch: char;
begin
    while not eof do begin
        while not eoln do begin
            read (Ch);
            if Ch = 'M'
                then writeln
                else begin
                    if Ch = 'x' then Ch := 'M';
                    write (Ch)
                end
        end;
        readln;
        write ('x')
    end
end.
```

16 • 'What's the input? (assume no line ends with punctuation)', 'what's the output?', 'write a program ...'

```
program PeriodReturn (input, output);
{Read and echo input.  In addition, print a carriage return after
each '.' and ','.}
var Ch: char;
begin
    while not eof do begin
        while not eoln do begin
            read (Ch);
            if Ch in ['.',',']
                then writeln (Ch)
                else write (Ch)
        end;
        writeln;
        readln
    end
end.
```

17 • 'What's the input? (assume no caps in input)', 'what's the output?'.

```
program Brackets (input, output);
{Starts capitalizing after seeing the second [, stops when the number of
] brackets equals the number of [ brackets.  Doesn't print the brackets.}
var Ch: char;
    Brackets: integer;
begin
    Brackets := 0;
    while not eof do begin
        read (Ch);
        if Ch = '[' then Brackets := Brackets + 1;
        if Ch = ']' then Brackets := Brackets - 1;
        if (Ch in ['a'..'z']) and (Brackets > 1) then
            Ch := chr((ord(Ch) - ord('a')) + ord('A'));
        if not (Ch in ['[',']']) then write (Ch)
    end
end.
```

18 • 'What's the input/output?', 'write a **program** ...', or change some conditions and make it 'where's the bug?'

```
program Braces (input, output);
{Capitalizes everything starting with first { after a [. Back to normal
at first } after a ]. Delimiters need not be adjacent. Prints all delimiters.}
var Ch: char;
     Brackets, Braces: boolean;
begin
   Brackets := false;
   Braces := false;
   while not eof do begin
      read (Ch);
      if Ch = '[' then Brackets := true;
      if (Ch = ']') and Braces then Brackets := false;
      if (Ch = '{') and Brackets then Braces := true;
      if (Ch = '}') and not Brackets then Braces := false;
      if Braces and (Ch in ['a'..'z']) then
         Ch := chr(ord(Ch) - ord('a') + ord('A'));
      write (Ch)
   end
end.
```

19 • 'What's the output?', 'what does it do?', or 'write a program ...'

```
program OneWordPerLine (input, output);
{Prints the first word from each input line. Ignore leading blanks.}
var Ch: char;
begin
   while not eof do begin
      read (Ch);
      while Ch = ' ' do
         read (Ch);
      while Ch <> ' ' do begin
         write (Ch);
         read (Ch)
      end;
      writeln;
      readln
   end
end.
```

20 • 'What's the output?', or introduce an error, and find the bug.

```
program TwoWords (input, output);
{Print the word that follows two words of the same length.}
var OldLength, NewLength: integer;
    Printing: boolean;
    Ch: char;
begin
   OldLength := MAXINT;
   Printing := false;
   while not eof do begin
      repeat
         read (Ch)
      until (Ch <> ' ') or eof; {skip leading blanks}
      if not eof then begin
         NewLength := 0;
         repeat
            NewLength := NewLength + 1;
            if Printing then write (Ch);
            read (Ch)
         until Ch = ' '
      end; {if not eof}
      if Printing then writeln;
      Printing := OldLength = NewLength;
      OldLength := NewLength
   end {while not eof}
end.
```

21 • 'Write a program ...', or move a line (esp. the readln) and find the bug.

```
program PeriodAlone (input, output);
{Echos text, preserving line structure. Spots lines that only contain a period.}
const Period = '.';
var Ch: char;
begin
   while not eof do begin
      if eoln
         then writeln
         else begin
            read (Ch);
            if (Ch = Period) and eoln
               then writeln ('Found it')
               else while not eoln do begin
                       write (Ch);
                       read (Ch)
                    end;
            writeln (Ch)
         end; {if not eoln}
      readln
   end
end.
```

22 • As above.

```
program PeriodLetter (input, output);
{Echos input, preserving line structure.  Spots any line that
contains a period followed by a single character (the 'command.')}
const Period = '.';
var Ch, Ch1: char;
begin
   while not eof do begin
      if eoln
         then writeln
         else begin
            read (Ch);
            if not eoln then begin
               read (Ch1);
               if (Ch = Period) and eoln
                  then writeln ('The command is ', Ch1)
                  else begin
                     write (Ch);
                     while not eoln do begin
                           write (Ch1);
                           read (Ch1);
                     end;
                     writeln (Ch1);
                  end {if Ch = Period...else}
            end  {not eoln after first character}
            else writeln (Ch)
         end {not eoln before first character}
      readln
   end {while not eof}
end.
```

23 • 'What's the input? (salt output with numbers)', 'what's the output?', or screw up an initialization and find the bug.

```
program TargetCount (input,output);
{Read and echo input.  In addition, count and report the number of times
the file's first letter appears on each line in the rest of the file.}
var Target, Ch: char;
    Count, Line: integer;
begin
   read (Target);
   write (Target);
   Line := 0;
   while not eof do begin
      Count := 0;
      Line := Line + 1;
      while not eoln do begin
         read (Ch);
         if Ch = Target then
            Count := Count + 1;
         write (Ch)
      end;
      writeln;
      writeln (Target, ' appeared ', Count, ' times on Line ', Line);
      readln
   end
end.
```

24 • 'What's the input?', 'write a program...', or induce bugs to look for as above, esp. removing checks.

```
program BlankCruncher (input, output);
{Echos input, maintaining line structure.  However, it crunches blanks, and
prints an in-line count of the blanks crunched.  Doesn't count eoln as a blank.}
var Ch: char;
    Blanks: integer;
begin
   Blanks := 0;
   while not eof do begin
      while not eoln do begin
         repeat
            read (Ch);
            if Ch = ' ' then Blanks := Blanks + 1
         until (Ch <> ' ') or eoln;
         if Blanks > 0 then write (Blanks:1);
         while (Ch <> ' ') and not eoln do begin
            write (Ch);
            read (Ch)
         end;
         if eoln
            then begin
               Blanks := 0;
               writeln (Ch)
            end
            else Blanks := 1
      end; {while not eoln}
      readln
   end {while not eof}
end.
```

Short responses ...

25 • Are these two code segments ever equivalent? Under what circumstances? [**equal for a non-blank line**]

```
repeat                          while not eoln do begin
   read (Ch);                      read (Ch);
   write (Ch)                      write (Ch)
until eoln;                     end;
```

26 • Is there any input for which these two segments of code are equivalent? What are its characteristics? [**equal if eof is not true when the segment begins.**]

```
repeat                          while not eof do
   while not eoln do               while not eoln do
      Process                         Process;
until eof;
```

27 • Is there any input for which these two code segments have the same effect? What are the characteristics of this input? [**equal if eof isn't true, and there are no blank lines.**]

```
repeat                          while not eof do
   repeat                          while not eoln do
      Process                         Process;
   until eoln
until eof;
```

28 • This program is supposed to read and add numbers. What problem will it face? [**crashes because eof isn't true after last number is read.**]

```
Sum := 0;
while not eof do begin
    read (Number);
    Sum := Sum + Number
end;
```

29 • What's wrong with this program segment? How would you correct it? Assume that Ch is a *char* variable.

```
read (Ch);
if Ch = eoln
    then writeln ('At the end of a line. ')
    else if Ch = eof
        then writeln ('At the end of the file. ')
```

30 • When are eof and eoln true?

31 • What is the last readable character in any text file? Why?

32 • A text file is known to contain *real* dollar amounts, along with other text. Each dollar amount is preceded by a dollar sign ($). This segment is supposed to add all the dollar amounts. Unfortunately, the program crashes. Why? Assume that Sum and Amount are *real* variables. [**there is a dollar sign that doesn't precede a number.**]

```
Sum := 0.0;
while not eof do begin
    read (Ch);
    if Ch = '$' then begin
        read (Amount);
        Sum := Sum + Amount
    end
end;
writeln (Sum);
```

33 • This program segment is supposed to print every other line of its text input; e.g. printing the first, third, fifth, etc., but ignoring the second, fourth, sixth, and so on. Unfortunately, it causes a program crash. Why? How would you fix it? [**crashes for odd number of input lines. Add check for eof before last readln.**]

```
while not eof do begin
    while not eoln do begin
        read (Ch);  write (Ch)
    end;
    readln;
    writeln;
    readln {discard the next line}
end;
```

34 • This program is supposed to add numbers. Unfortunately, it crashes on some input files. Why? [**reads a leading non-number or non-blank**]

```
Sum := 0;
while not eof do begin
    readln (Number);
    Sum := Sum + Number
end;
writeln (Sum);
```

35 • This program segment is supposed to read and echo text. What's wrong with it? [**does't echo the last character of each line, also, prints an empty line as a space preceding the next line.**]

```
while not eof do begin
   read (Ch);
   while not eoln do begin
      write (Ch);
      read (Ch)
   end;
   readln;
   writeln
end;
```

36 • This program is supposed to print the first character of the first input line, the second character of the second line, and so on for ten lines of input. Unfortunately, it doesn't seem to work for some inputs. How come? [**lines may be too short**]

```
i := 1;
while not eof and (i < = 10) do begin
   for j := 1 to i do
      read (Ch);
   write (Ch);
   readln;
   i := i + 1
end;
writeln;
```

Write a program that ...

37 • Write a program that counts the number of spaces, but not end-of-lines, in a sample of input text.

38 • Write a program that reads and echos text, obeying the following special rule: if a line of text ends with an ampersand (&), join it to the next line.

39 • Write a program that reads and echos text, obeying this special: do not print vowels, except when the vowel appears at the beginning of a word.

40 • Write a program that reads and echos text, but modifies certain characters or character pairs so that the text is printed with an Argentinian accent. Rules are: double 'l' or single 'y' are printed as 'j', 'z' is printed as an 's', and 'd' is printed as 'th'. For a Uruguayan twist, print 's' and 'c' as 'ch'. Assume that all input is lower-case.

41 • Write a program that reads and echos text. Assume that repeated characters have been compressed according to the following rule: a run of characters is printed as a backslash, followed by the character, and the number of times it should occur. Print the text in uncompressed form.

42 • Write a program that reads text, and prints the number of letters in each word. Don't print the words themselves, but maintain line structure when you print the counts.

43 • Write a program that decrypts its input. Assume that every nth character is junk (and should not be echoed). The value of n is 2 plus the remainder left when the number of characters on the previous line is divided by 4, Assume that the first line of input has no junk characters.

44 • Write a program that counts the number of completely blank lines in input.

45 • A file contains an unnamed professor's class accounts. Each line in the file consists of a letter grade ('A', 'B', or 'C'), the dollar and cent amount paid for the grade, and the student's name. A typical line is:

    C$20.00 Debbie Estrogen

Note that there are no spaces between the grade and its price, and only a single space between the price and the name. Write a program that prints the name of each student who has purchased a grade, the most frequently given grade, and the average price overall.

Chapter Nine

Understanding code ...

1 • What is the proper order of a program's parts?

       procedure or function declarations
       program heading
       statement part
       type definitions
       variable declarations
       constant definitions

2 • What are the values of each of these expressions? 'Error' is one possible value. Assume these definitions, declarations, and assignments:

    type Motown = (Smokey, Marvin, Temptations, Supremes);
           GirlGroups = (Shirelles, Ronnettes, Crystals);
    var Soul: Motown;
        Top40: GirlGroups;
    Soul := Smokey;
    Top40 := Crystals;

Soul	GirlGroups
succ (Soul)	pred (Top40)
succ (Top40)	pred (Soul)
ord (Motown)	ord (Top40)
ord (Smokey)	ord (succ(Soul))
Soul < >GirlGroups	Smokey = Marvin

3 • Which pairs of these enumerated type definitions could appear in a single program? [a − c, b − d]

    a)   Weekday = (Monday, Tuesday, Wednesday, Thursday, Friday);
    b)   PokerNights = (Thursday, Tuesday);
    c)   Weekend = (Saturday, Sunday);
    d)   LongWeekend = (Friday, Saturday, Sunday);

4 • Which of these are legal definitions? [a, e, f]

    a)   Short = 1..10;
    b)   Brief = (1, 2, 3, 4, 5, 6, 7, 8, 9, 10);
    c)   Monogram = ('D', 'B', 'C');
    d)   Initials = ('B', 'C', 'D');
    e)   ForShort = (B, C, D);
    f)   Boring = 'A'..'A';

5 • Suppose we make the definitions and declarations shown below. Which of the assignments are always in error, sometimes in error, or never in error?

    type Low = 1..7;
        Mid = 5..10;
        High = 11..20;
        Broad = 1..20;
    var LowValue: Low;
       MidValue: Mid;
       HighValue: High;
       BroadValue: Broad;

    a)   LowValue := 2 * MidValue; [**always**]
    b)   MidValue := LowValue; [**sometimes**]
    c)   BroadValue := HighValue; [**never**]
    d)   HighValue := BroadValue; [**sometimes**]
    e)   MidValue := 3 * HighValue; [**always**]

6 • Suppose that we make the definitions and declarations shown below. Which of the pairs of headings and calls are always in error, sometimes in error, and never in error?

```
type Low = 1..7;
     Mid = 5..10;
     High = 11..20;
     Broad = 1..20;
var LowValue: Low;
    MidValue: Mid;
    HighValue: High;
    BroadValue: Broad;
```

a) procedure Test (Param: Low); [**sometimes**]
    Test (MidValue);
b) procedure Exam (var Arg: Mid); [**always**]
    Exam (LowValue);
c) procedure Quiz (Value: 1..7); [**always**]
    Quiz (LowValue);
d) procedure Help (Variable: integer); [**never**]
    Help (HighValue);
e) procedure Confuse (var What: integer); [**always**]
    Confuse (HighValue);

Short responses ...

7 • What is an ordinal type? What simple type is not ordinal? What does it mean to say that a type is enumerable?

8 • What are the constants of an ordinal type? How do they differ from programmer-defined constants?

9 • How would you describe the relationship between the type of a variable parameter and the type of its argument? Give a legal and illegal example.

10 • How would you describe the relationship between the type of a value parameter and the type of its argument? Give an example that is always legal, one that is sometimes legal, and one that is never legal.

11 • The text claims that 'relying on run-time crashes to do error checking is like using telephone poles (instead of brakes) to stop your car.' What kind of run-time crashes are being referred to? Despite this advice, do we ever build the possiblity of run-time crashes into programs on purpose? Why?

12 • Suppose that *Value* is a variable with an enumerated ordinal type? Are either of these statements ever legal? Why or why not?

```
read (Value);
writeln (Value);
```

Write a program that ...

13 • Suppose that we've made this type definition:

```
type NickNames = (Boss, BigBopper, Killer, MainMan);
```

Write a procedure that takes a parameter of type NickNames, and prints its value.

Chapter Eleven

Understanding code ...

1 • Where's the bug? [**missing five is reported in position 20**]

```
{find the five in a 20-element array}
Position := 1;
while (Position < 20) and (Storage[Position] < > 5) do
    Position := Position + 1;
writeln ('The five is in element ', Position);
```

2 • Where's the bug? [**out of range error for missing 7**]

```
{find the seven in a 20-element array}
Position := 1;
while Storage[Position]<>7  do
    Position := Position + 1;
writeln ('The seven is in element ', Position);
```

3 • Suppose that we make these definitions:

```
const MAXROW = 5;
      MAXCOL = 7;
type Game = array [1..MAXROW, 1..MAXCOL] of char;
var Board:  Game;
    i, j: integer;
```

Imagine that *Board* has been suitably initialized.   Which of these loops is illegal? [**d**]

```
a) for i := MAXROW downto 1 do            b) for j := 1 to MAXCOL do
       for j := 1 to MAXCOL do                   for i := 1 to MAXROW do
           writeln (Board [i, j]);                   writeln (Board [i, j]);


c) for j := 1 to MAXROW do               d) for i := 1 to MAXROW do
       for i := 1 to MAXROW do                   for j := 1 to MAXCOL do
           writeln (Board [j, i]);                   writeln (Board [j, i]);
```

4 • Which of these are legal type definitions? [**bcehi**]

```
a)      type Perhaps = array packed [1..20] of char;
b)      type Maybe = packed array [0..20] of char;
c)      type Question  = array ['0'..'9'] of integer;
d)      type IDunno = array [1.0..15.0] of real;
e)      type Why = array [1..10, 'a'..'z'] of real;
f)      type Who = array ['1','2','3','4','5'] of char;
g)      type Where = array [integer] of char;
h)      type When = array [char] of integer;
i)      type WhyNot = array [boolean] of char;
```

5 • What is the size of each of these arrays? In other words, how many elements could be stored in a variable of each array type?

```
a)      type Holder  = array [0..20] of integer;  [21]
b)      type Data = array [1..5, 1..12] of char;  [60]
c)      type Count = array ['a'..'z', 'A'..'Z'] of integer;  [676]
d)      type Funny = array ['c'..'f', '1'..'9'] of real;  [36]
e)      type Monopoly = array [1..8, 1..8, 1..8, 1..8] of char;  [4096]
f)      type  Really = array [−4..9] of real;  [14]
```

6 • Which of the statements below are legal, given the following **type** and **var** declarations? [a]

```
type String = packed array [1..20] of char;
     Large = array [char] of char;
     Data = array [1..20] of integer;
var Thin, Thick: String;
    Alpha: Large;
    Better: Data;
```

a) Thin := Thick;

b) Thin['a'] := Alpha['#'];

c) Thick['3'] := Alpha['b'];

d) writeln (String);

e) writeln (Alpha);

f) Large['c'] := Thick[2];

g) Alpha := Thick;

h) Better := Thin;

7 • Which of the following assignment statements are illegal? Circle the error, if there is one. Assume these definitions and declarations. In the examples, assume that variables have been defined where necessary. [a−d]

```
type Data = array [1..20, 'a'..'z'] of char;
     String = packed array [1..40] of char;
     WhyNot = array [1..40] of integer;

var First, Second: Data;
    Long: String;
    Why: WhyNot;
```

a)   First[pred(1), 'a'] := Second[1, 'a'];

b)   Long := First[1..20];

c)   First[Why[1], Long[1]] := String[1];

d)   Long[Why[3]] := Why[Long[3]];

e)   Why[sqr(3)] := 4;

f)   Long[First[1, 'a] := 'a';

g)   Why[(2*4) div 4] := ord(Long[2]);

8 • Where's the bug? [**Uses read as red herring. Needs char-by-char input.**]

```
program StringInput (input, output);
{Compares two strings for equality.}
type String = packed array [1..10] of char;
var FirstWord, SecondWord: String;
begin
    writeln ('Enter two words, one per line, exactly 10 character long each. ');
    read (FirstWord);
    read (SecondWord);
    if FirstWord = SecondWord
        then writeln ('They were the same. ')
        else writeln ('They were different. ')
end.
```

9 • What's the bug? [**missing subscripts**]

```
program ArrayUser (input, output);
{Reads in 10 values, then prints them in reverse order.}
type TenValues = array [1..10] of integer;
var i: integer;
    Hold: TenValues;
begin
    writeln ('This program reads 10 integers, then prints ');
    writeln ('them in reverse order.  Please enter the 10 integers. ');
    for i := 1 to 10 do
        read (Hold);
    for i := 10 downto 1 do
        write (Hold);
    writeln
end.
```

10 • Where's the bug? Is it a compile-time or run-time bug? [**array defined 10..40. Run-time bug.**]

```
program Reverse (input, output);
{Reverses 30 chars worth of input.}
type ShortLine = array [10..40] of char;
var i: integer;
    Letters: ShortLine;
begin
  writeln ('Please enter 30 chars worth of input. ');
  for i := 1 to 30 do
    read (Letters[(30-i) + 1]);
  for i := 1 to 30 do
    write (Letters[i]);
  writeln
end.
```

11 • Where's the bug? Compile-time or run-time? [**compile-time, tries to set array bound at run-time**]

```
program ReverseChars (input, output);
{Stores, then echos in reverse, characters entered by the user.}
type Hold = packed array [1..HowMany] of char;
var Store: Hold;
    i, HowMany: integer;
begin
  writeln ('How many chararacters do you want to reverse? ');
  readln (HowMany);
  for i := 1 to HowMany do
    read (Store[i]);
  writeln ('In reverse, you entered ');
  for i := HowMay downto 1 do
    write (Store[i]);
  writeln
end.
```

12 • Where's the bug? Run-time or compile-time? How do you fix it? [**Compile-time type clash in last write, fix with chr formula.**]

```
program ArrayDigitCounter (input, output);
{Counts the number of times each digit appears in a sequence of digits.}
type Totals = array ['0'..'9'] of integer;
var Digits: Totals;
    CurrentDigit: char;
    Count, Limit: integer;
begin
  for CurrentDigit := '0' to '9' do
    Digits[CurrentDigit] := 0;
  writeln ('How many digits are you going to enter? ');
  readln (Limit);
  writeln ('Please enter the digits ');
  for Count := 1 to Limit do begin
    read (CurrentDigit);
    Digits[CurrentDigit] := Digits[CurrentDigit] + 1
  end;
  writeln ('The number of times each digit occured was ');
  for Limit := 0 to 9 do
    write (Limit, Digits[Limit]);
  writeln
end.
```

13 • 'What's the output?', 'write a program ...', 'where's the bug? (make it (MAX div 2) +1))', 'modify this program (to add second to first, third to second, etc.), (to add first to second, second to third, etc.)'

```
program  Numbers (input,output);
{Initializes a one-dimensional  array.  Adds first element to second, third
to fourth, etc.  Prints array.}
const MAX = 10;
type Source  = array [1..MAX] of integer;
var Data:  Source;
     i:  integer;
begin
   writeln ('Please enter ', MAX, ' integers ');
   for i := 1 to MAX do
      read (Data[i]);
   for i := 1 to (MAX div 2) do
      Data[2*i] := Data[2*i] + Data[2*i − 1];
   for i := 1 to MAX do
      write (Data[i])
end.
```

14 • 'What's the output?', 'where's the bug (change exit condition, confuse Current with Next).'

```
program Jumper (input, output);
{Initialize a one-D array.  Then, starting at the first element, set the
element to zero, and move to the element that its former value subscripted.
Continue until an out-of-range subscript is requested.}
const MAX = 10;
type Source  = array [1..MAX] of integer;
var Data:  Source;
     Current, Next, i:  integer;
begin
   for i := 1 to MAX do
      read (Data[i]);
   readln;
   Current := 1;
   repeat
      Next := Data[Current];
      Data[Current] := 0;
      Current := Next
   until (Current > MAX) or (Current < 1);
   for i := 1 to MAX do
      write (Data[i]);
   writeln
end.
```

15 • Here's the input, what's the output?   [**reverses the input**]

```
program Flip (input, output);
const MAX = 10;
type Data = array [1..MAX] of integer;
var Store:Data;
    i, j:integer;
procedure Switch (var Element1, Element2: integer);
  var Temp: integer;
  begin
    Temp := Element1;
    Element1 := Element2;
    Element2 := Temp
  end;
begin
  for i := 1 to MAX do
    read (Store[i]);
  readln;
  for i := 1 to (MAX div 2) do begin
    j := 2*i;
    Switch (Store[j], Store[MAX − j + 1])
  end;
  for i := 1 to MAX do
    write (Store[i]);
  writeln
end.
```

16 • 'What's the output?', 'where's the bug?', 'write a program...'

```
program TheMost (input, output);
{Reads text, and prints the line that contains the most instances of 'a'.}
const TARGET = 'a';
      MAX = 80;
type Line = packed array [1..MAX] of char;
var Most, Current: Line;
    i, TargetCount, MostCount: integer;
begin
  writeln ('Please enter your text. ');
  MostCount := −MAXINT;
  Most := 0;
  while not eof do begin
    for i := 1 to MAX do
      Current[i] := ' ';
    TargetCount := 0;
    i := 0;
    while not eoln and (i < 80) do begin
      i := i + 1;
      read (Current[i]);
      if Current[i] = TARGET then TargetCount := TargetCount + 1
    end; {eoln}
    readln;
    if TargetCount > MostCount then begin
      Most := Current;
      MostCount := TargetCount
    end {then}
  end; {eof}
  writeln (Most)
end.
```

17 • 'What's the input?', 'what's the output?', 'write procedure Shift,' 'where's the bug? (by introducing an error into Shift),' 'how long should MAX be to make output the same as input? [TIMES].'

```
program Marquee (input, output);
{Rotates the contents of a one-dimensional array to the right, one element at
a time (like a theater marquee), TIMES times. Wraps from MAX to first.}
const MAX = 10;
      TIMES = 5;
type String = packed array [1..MAX] of char;
var Long: String;
    i: integer;
procedure Shift (var Short: String; Size: integer);
   var i: integer;
       Temp: char;
   begin
     Temp := Short[Size];
     for i := Size downto 2 do
        Short[i] := Short[i-1];
     Short[1] := Temp
   end;
begin
   i := 0;
   while not eoln and (i < MAX) do begin
     i := i + 1;
     read (Long[i])
   end;
   for i := (i + 1) to MAX do
     Long[i] := ' ';
   for i := 1 to TIMES do
     Shift (Long, MAX);
   for i := 1 to MAX do
     write (Long[i]);
   writeln
end.
```

18 • 'What's the output?', 'where's the bug? (don't reinitialize Current to blanks, don't readln after each input line)', 'modify this program (so that as long as the three MARKERS occur in the first MAX characters, the whole line will be printed)'.

```
program PrintSomeLines (input, output);
{Read text, and print only those lines with three or more MARKERS.
Assume 60 characters per line, maximum.}
const MARKER = 'e';
      MAX = 60;
type Line = packed array [1..MAX] of char;
var Current: Line;
    MarkCount, Counter: integer;
begin
   while not eof do begin
     for Counter := 1 to MAX do
        Current[Counter] := ' ';
     Counter := 1;
     MarkCount := 0;
     while not eoln and (Counter <= MAX) do begin
        read (Current[Counter]);
        if (Current[Counter] = MARKER) then
           MarkCount := MarkCount + 1;
        Counter := Counter + 1
     end;
     if MarkCount > 2 then writeln (Current);
     readln
   end
end.
```

19 • 'What's the input?', 'where's the bug?,' 'write a program ...'

```
program NumberAdder (input,output);
{Initialize as follows:  for two odd or even subscripts, read the value; for
exactly one odd subscript, element gets their difference.  Print the array.}
const ROW = 5;
      COL = 9;
type Source = array[1..ROW, 1..COL] of integer;
var Data:  Source;
    i,j:  integer;
begin
   for i := 1 to ROW do
      for j := 1 to COL do
         if odd(i+j)
            then Data [i,j] := i−j
            else read (Data [i,j]);
   for i := 1 to ROW do begin
      for j := 1 to COL do
         write (Data [i,j]);
      writeln
   end
end.
```

20 • 'What's the input?', 'what's the output?', 'modify to print individual lines (or every other line) in proper order,' 'modify to avoid printing blank lines or unnecessary blanks on any given line (assume no leading blanks on any input line),' 'where's the bug?'

```
program Backward (input, output);
{Read a text file, print the file, and each line, in reverse order.}
const MAXLINE = 40;
      MAXPAGE = 20;
type Line = array [1..MAXLINE] of char;
     Page = array [1..MAXPAGE] of Line;
var Whole:  Page;
    ChNum, LineNum, i, j:  integer;
begin
   LineNum := 0;
   while not eof and (LineNum < MAXPAGE) do begin
      LineNum := LineNum + 1;
      ChNum := 0;
      while not eoln and (ChNum < MAXLINE) do begin
         ChNum := ChNum + 1;
         read (Whole[LineNum][ChNum])
      end;
      readln
   end;
   for i := LineNum downto 1 do begin
      for j := MAXLINE downto 1 do
         write (Whole[i][j]);
      writeln
   end
end.
```

21 • 'What's the input?,' 'what's the output?,' write one of the procedures, 'where's the bug? (some possibilities are shown),' 'what does it do?' (make it more cryptic first).

```
program Rotated (input, output);
{Read two small arrays, and decide if one is a rotation of the other.}
const MAX = 3;
type Matrix = array[1..MAX, 1..MAX] of integer;
var First, Second:  Matrix;
     i, j, Count:  integer;
function SameArray (One, Two:  Matrix):  boolean;
   var i, j:  integer;
        Match:  boolean;
   begin
      Match := true;
      for i := 1 to MAX do
         for j := 1 to MAX do
            if One[i,j] < > Two[i,j] then
               Match := false;
            {Change to 'Match := One[i,j] = Two[i,j]' for a hard bug}
      SameArray := Match
   end;
procedure Ninety (var Board:  Matrix);
   var Temp:  Matrix;
   begin
      for i := 1 to MAX do
         for j := 1 to MAX do
            Temp[i,j] := Board [(MAX−j)+1, i];
         {Change to 'Board [j, i]' for a good bug.}
      Board := Temp
   end;
procedure ReadArray (var Bored:Matrix);
   var i,j:  integer;
   begin
      writeln ('Please enter a ', MAX, ' by ', MAX, ' array. ');
      for i := 1 to MAX do begin
         for j := 1 to MAX do
            read (Bored[i,j]);
         readln
      end
   end;
begin
   ReadArray (First);
   ReadArray (Second);
   Count := 0;
   while (Count < 4) and not SameArray (First, Second) do begin
      Ninety (First);
      Count := Count + 1
   end;
   if SameArray (First, Second)
      then writeln ('They are equal after ', Count, ' clockwise rotations. ')
      else writeln ('They are not equivalent. ')
end.
```

22 • 'What's the output?', 'what does it do?', 'where's the bug? (forget to reinitialize lines, forget to readln, screw up counts, change 'if ChNum=21 then ... else ...' to 'Current[ChNum] := ´ ´ (a bug if input line is exactly 20 characters), make the final 'writeln (Last)' a writeln (Current)' instead)' 'modify this program (don't bother creating Last, change maximum output line length).'

```
program Joiner (input, output);
{A moronic text justifier. Repeatedly reads line Current, then stuffs it
into line Last if it won't make Last overflow. When Last is 'full' (i.e. can't
hold another input line) it gets printed.}
const MAX = 20;
type Line = array [1..MAX] of char;
var Current, Last:  Line;
    LastLength, ChNum, i:  integer;
begin
   for i := 1 to MAX do      {initialize the holding array to blanks}
      Last[i] := ´ ´;
   LastLength := 0;
   while not eof do begin
      ChNum := 1;
      for i := 1 to MAX do  {initialize the current line to blanks}
         Current[i] := ´ ´;
      while not eoln and (ChNum <= MAX) do begin
         read (Current[ChNum]);
         ChNum := ChNum + 1  {read the new input into Current}
      end;
      if ChNum = 21   {put in a space to avoid mashing lines if it will fit}
         then ChNum := 20
         else Current[ChNum] := ´ ´;
      readln;
      if (ChNum + LastLength) <= MAX
         then begin
            for i := 1 to ChNum do  {Add Current to Last}
               Last[i + LastLength] := Current[i];
            LastLength := LastLength + ChNum
         end
         else begin
            writeln (Last);  {or, print Last, then save Current}
            Last := Current;
            LastLength := ChNum
         end
   end;
   writeln (Last)      {The last line still needs to be written out}
end.
```

Short responses ...

23 • Suppose that we're going to be counting capital letters in text input. What are the relative advantages of each of these array type definitions?

```
Count = array [´A´..´Z´] of integer;
Track = array [char] of integer;
```

24 • What's the difference between an array of *char* values, and an array subscripted by *char* values?

25 • Write the code needed to initialize an array, subscripted by the type *char*, assuming a 256 character collating sequence.

26 • What is a random access type? Is the array type the only random access type? Are simple-typed variables random access?

27 • What are three special rules that must be followed in defining a string type?

28 • What special characteristics do the string types have? How do they differ from ordinary arrays?

29 • What is the difference between these definitions? What effect will this have on variables of these types?

```
type Verb = packed array [2..5] of char;
     Noun = packed array [1..4] of char;
```

30 • What does this error message mean? Give an example that would cause the error.

   SUBSCRIPT OUT OF RANGE

31 • Is this a legal heading? Why or why not?

   procedure Sort (var List: array [1..10] of integer);

32 • What is a structured type? What Pascal types are not structured?

33 • What is the difference between these two type definitions?

   High = array [1..5, 6..10] of integer;
   Low = array [1..10] of integer;

34 • Can the proper length for an array be computed at run-time (e.g. not until the program actually executes) in Pascal?

35 • Suppose that a program contains two array-typed variables (call them *First* and *Second*). Under what conditions is the assignment *First* := *Second* legal? (Hint: there is more than one possibility.)

36 • The array defined below is supposed to be subscripted only by the low odd numbers. Is it a legal definition? Why or why not?

   type Odds = array [1, 3, 5, 7, 9] of integer;

37 • Describe briefly, in words, a linear search, a quadratic search, and a binary search of an array.

Write a program that ...

38 • Write a program that prints every other occurrence of each capital letter; i.e. every other 'A', every other 'B,' etc.

39 • Write a program that counts letters, and prints the three most frequent ones (most frequent upper-case, lower-case, three of each).

40 • Write a procedure that reverses a 45 (or try 46) character string.

41 • Write a procedure that initializes the odd elements of a one-dimensional array subscripted by the capital letters to 1, and the even elements to −1.

42 • Write a procedure that initializes the elements of a three dimensional array in the following manner: if the sum of the subscripts is odd, initialize the element to 0, otherwise initialize the element to *MAXINT*.

43 • Write a procedure that initializes the elements of a two dimensional array in the following manner: elements above the upper-left–lower-right diagonal should be set to 1, those below the diagonal should get −1, and those on the diagonal should be initialized to 0.

44 • Write a function that (detects the presence of) (finds the position of) a five-character pattern in a one-dimensional string *MAX* characters long (or in an array of these strings).

45 • Write a procedure that interleaves two arrays, element-by-element, into an array twice as long.

46 • Write a procedure that find the largest and smallest values in a four-dimensional array, along with their positions.

47 • Write a procedure that finds the element, in a two-dimensional array, that is closest in value to the upper-left element.

Chapter Twelve

Understanding code ...

1 • Is this definition legal or illegal?

```
type Hold = record
              Hold: integer
            end;
```

2 • Is this definition legal or illegal?

```
type Hold = record
              Hold: integer;
              Hold: real;
            end;
```

3 • Is this definition and declaration legal or illegal?

```
type Hold = record
              {field definitions}
            end;
     var Hold: Hold;
```

4 • Is this definition and declaration legal or illegal?

```
type Hold = record
              Save: integer
            end;
     var Save: Hold;
```

5 • Are these definitions legal or illegal?

```
type Hold = record
              Save: integer
            end;
     Save = record
              Save: Hold
            end;
```

6 • Suppose that we have this definition and declaration:

```
type Hold = record
              Data1, Data2: integer
            end;
     var Rec1, Rec2: Hold;
```

What are the final values of Rec1 and Rec2 after these assignments?

[Rec1.Data1	Rec1.Data2	Rec2.Data1	Rec2.Data2
a) **undefined**	**undefined**	1	2
b) **1**	**2**	**undefined**	**undefined**
c) **undefined**	**undefined**	1	2
d) **1**	**2**	**undefined**	**undefined**]

```
a)   with Rec1, Rec2 do begin         b)   with Rec1, Rec2 do begin
       Data1 := 1;                            Rec1.Data1 := 1;
       Data2 := 2                             Rec1.Data2 := 2
     end;                                   end;


c)   with Rec1, Rec2 do begin         d)   with Rec2 do begin
       Rec2.Data1 := 1;                       Rec1.Data1 := 1;
       Data2 := 2                             Rec1.Data2 := 2
     end;                                   end;
```

NOTE: As you have probably found on your own tests, record questions tend either to focus on syntax (and be too simple), or to require manipulation of large data structures (and require an excessive amount of code to be stated as problems). I am open to suggestions, and will happily pay $10.00 for any 'understanding code' or 'short response' record questions that I can use in the next installment of this manual. In the meantime, I hope that some of the questions that follow will prove useful.

Write a program that ...

The next group of questions refer to this data type definition:

```
type Generation = (Unborn, First, Second);
     Community = record
                       Age: Generation;
                       Occupants: integer
                 end;
     Land = array [1..49, 1..49] of Community;
var Board: Land;
```

7 • Write a procedure that initializes *Board*. It should read the coordinates of individual elements, and settle each with a single first-generation occupant. All other elements should be given zero unborn occupants.

8 • Write a procedure that is given the location of a single element, and modifies it according to these rules: double the number of its occupants if it is second generation, make it second generation if it is first generation, leave it alone if it is unborn.

9 • Write a procedure that displays the contents of a board, indicating generation and number of occupants (if occupied).

10 • Write a procedure that will move the occupants of an element to an adjoining unoccupied element. Follow this rule for searching: up, right, down, left. Print an error message if no adjoining element is available.

11 • Write a procedure that simulates the effect of a tactical nuclear weapon: obliterate the population of a given element (setting its generation to unborn), and reduce by one-half (rounding down) the population of each of the eight neighboring elements.

12 • Write a procedure that will add the occupants of an element to the adjoining element with the lowest current occupancy. Advance the generation of the 'invaded' element from unborn to first, or from first to second.

13 • Write a procedure that sets the generation of an element to unborn, and its contents to zero, if the eight elements that surround it are all in their second generation *or* have a total population in excess of thirty.

14 • Suppose that the board 'tilts' to the right so sharply that occupants begin to slide! Write a procedure that, starting at the far left end of each row, moves half (rounding up) of each element's occupants one element to the right. Follow this special rule: If the new population of an element exceeds ten, kill its occupants and and make it unborn. Otherwise, leave the element's generation alone.

The next group of questions refer to this data type definition:

```
const SIZE = 9;
type Color = (White, Brown);
     Inhabitant = (Red, Black, None, Edge);
     Checks = record
                    Square: Color;
                    Owner: Inhabitant
              end;
     Board = array [0..SIZE, 0..SIZE] of Checks;
var Checkers: Board;
```

15 • Write a procedure that initializes a board to the start of a game of checkers. (Remember that only one color square is used to play!)

16 • Write a procedure that determines the safety of an occupied square. Do not worry about kings or jumps. Print the location of threatening squares.

17 • Write a procedure that is given a paticular piece and position, then decides a) what moves can be made from that position, and b) which of the moves are safe. Do not worry about kings or jumps.

18 • Write a procedure that determines what jumps, if any, can be made from a given player's position. Do not worry about multiple jumps. Print the positions of pieces that can be jumped.

19 • Write a procedure that determines what *double* jumps, if any, can be made from a given player's

position. Print the positions of pieces that can be jumped.

20 • Write a procedure that moves a given player's piece and updates the board. Supply the starting position and desired ending position as arguments. If the move is illegal, print an error message and leave the board alone.

21 • Write a procedure that moves a given player's checker, if possible. It does not matter which of several possible moves is taken, as long as a single jump is made if possible. If a move cannot be made, print an error message, otherwise update the board.

22 • Write a procedure that is given the position of a king (which can move either forward or backward), and determines a) what moves it can make, and b) what single jumps it can make. Print the locations of all legal moves.

The following questions can be presented in a similar manner: provide a data type definition, then ask for manipulation routines.

General chess problems:

23 • Initialize the board (for both players) (starting with a board in any orientation).

24 • Print the current configuration of a chessboard.

25 • Determine the safety of a particular piece (threatened by a given piece on an otherwise empty board) (threatened by a given piece on a board with other pieces).

26 • Decide if a given piece endangers any other piece.

27 • Determine whether or not a piece is protected (like being endangered, but by a piece from the same side).

28 • Confirms the outcome of a proposed move: legal, illegal, takes a piece.

29 • Print legal moves of a given piece (assuming an empty board) (assuming that its progress may be blocked) (assuming that it may take another piece).

30 • Compare the relative value of possible pawn moves (which move takes the highest-value opponent?).

31 • Finds the piece closest to a given piece along a particular diagonal or horizontal path.

32 • Determine if a king can legally castle (and make the move).

Some assorted data-structuring problems:

33 • Define a data type suitable for representing a Monopoly board. (What are the primitive operations liable to be associated with a Monopoly data structure?)

34 • Define a data type for representing a deck of cards. (Consider application to different card games.)

35 • Define a data type that could be used in an address book program. Keep track of name, area code and phone number, address, city, state, zip code.

36 • Define a data type for keeping student records. Keep track of each student's name, major, GPA, birthdate, social security number.

Chapter Thirteen

Understanding code ...

1 • Find the bug: [**Data isn't declared as a variable.**]

```
program Bugs (input, Data);
{Put the first line of input into file Data.}
var Ch: char;
begin
   rewrite (Data);
   while not eoln do begin
      read (Ch);
      write (Data, Ch)
   end;
   writeln (Data)
end.
```

2 • Find the bug: [**Can't read directly to Data.**]

```
program Bugs (input, Data);
{Put the first line of input into file Data.}
var Ch: char;
    Data: text;
begin
   rewrite (Data);
   while not eoln do
      read (Data, Ch)
end.
```

3 • Where's the bug? [**reset should be rewrite.**]

```
program Bugs (output, Data);
{Print the contents of Data.}
var Ch: char;
    Data: text;
begin
   rewrite (Data);
   while not eof (Data) do begin
      while not eoln (Data) do begin
         read (Data, Ch);
         write (Ch)
      end;
      readln (Data);
      writeln
   end
end.
```

4 • Where's the bug? [**write and writeln should not refer to Data**]

```
program Bugs (output, Data);
{Print the contents of Data.}
var Ch: char;
    Data: text;
begin
   reset (Data);
   while not eof (Data) do begin
      while not eoln (Data) do begin
         read (Data, Ch);
         write (Data, Ch)
      end;
      readln (Data);
      writeln (Data)
   end
end.
```

5 • Where's the bug? [**eof and eoln should have Data as arguments.**]

```
program Bugs (output, Data);
{Print the contents of Data.}
var Ch: char;
    Data: text;
begin
  reset (Data);
  while not eof do begin
    while not eoln do begin
      read (Data, Ch);
      write (Ch)
    end;
    readln (Data);
    writeln
  end
end.
```

6 • Which of these types of values can't be stored in a textfile? [**b, c, f**]

a)	integer		b)	record
c)	array		d)	real
e)	file		f)	enumerated ordinal types

7 • What are the contents of file *Test* after each sequence? The responses 'Error' or 'Test is unchanged' are possibilities.

```
reset (Test);                     [Error]
writeln (Test, 'Hi there ');


rewrite (Test);                   [Hi there]
writeln (Test, 'Hi there ');


rewrite (Test);                   [Hi there]
writeln (Test, 'Hi there ');
rewrite (Test);
writeln (Test, 'Hi there ');


rewrite (Test);                   [Hi there]
writeln (Test, 'Hi there ');
reset (Test);
```

8 • What's the output? The contents of Data are: Hi John. The input supplied to the program is: Hi Jane. [**JJ**]

```
program Exam (input, output, Data);
var Ch1, Ch2: char;
    Data: text;
begin
  reset (Data);
  if not eof and not eof (Data) then
    while input ↑ = Data ↑ do begin
      read (Ch1);
      read (Data, Ch2)
    end;
  writeln (Ch1, Ch2)
end.
```

9 • What's the output? The contents of Data are: james dean. The input supplied to the program is: rebel without a cause. [**em**]

```
program Exam (input, output, Data);
var Ch1, Ch2: char;
    Data: text;
begin
  reset (Data);
  read (Ch1);
  while Ch1 < > Data ↑ do begin
    read (Ch1);
    read (Data, Ch2)
  end;
  writeln (Ch1, Ch2)
end.
```

10 • What's the output? [**merges Data and Facts on output: two characters from Facts, one from Data. Cleans up any remainder.**]

```
program Exam (output, Data, Facts);
var Ch1, Ch2, Ch3: char;
    Data, Facts: text;
begin
  reset (Facts);
  reset (Data);
  while not eof (Facts) and not eof (Data) do begin
    read (Facts, Ch1);
    read (Data, Ch2);
    if not eof (Facts) then read (Facts, Ch3);
    write (Ch1, Ch3, Ch2)
  end;
  while not eof (Facts) do begin
    read (Facts, Ch1);
    write (Ch1)
  end;
  while not eof (Data) do begin
    read (Data, Ch2);
    write (Ch2)
  end;
  writeln
end.
```

11 • What's the output? [**Prints odd-numbered lines of Facts, and even-numbered lines of Data. Doesn't housekeep any remainder.**]

```
program Exam (output, Data, Facts);
var Ch: char;
    Data, Facts: text;
begin
  reset (Facts);
  reset (Data);
  if not eof (Data) then readln (Data);
  while not eof (Facts) and not eof (Data) do begin
    while not eoln (Facts) do begin
      read (Facts, Ch);
      write (Ch)
    end;
    writeln;
    while not eoln (Data) do begin
      read (Data, Ch);
      write (Ch)
    end;
    writeln;
    readln (Facts);
    readln (Data);
    if not eof (Facts) then readln (Facts);
    if not eof (Data) then readln (Data);
  end
end.
```

12 • What does this program do? [**inspects Data, puts odd numbers into Low, evens into High.**]

```
program Test (Data, Low, High);
type Numbers = file of integer;
var Data, Low, High: Numbers;
begin
  reset (Data);
  rewrite (Low);
  rewrite (High);
  while not eof (Data) do begin
    if odd (Data ↑ )
      then put (Low, Data ↑ )
      else put (High, Data ↑ )
    get (Data)
  end
end.
```

Short responses ...

13 • What is the difference between internal and external files?

14 • What is a textfile? What does it contain? Does Pascal consider textfiles to be different from other files? In what ways (e.g. what required procedures are only defined for textfiles)?

15 • What is the file window? Why is it useful? What procedures are used to manipulate it?

16 • What are the effects of procedures *reset* and *rewrite* ?

17 • Can *read* and *write* be used with all file type? What about *readln* and *writeln* ?

18 • What is a sequential access data type?

19 • Suggest three applications in which files are more suitable than arrays. Three for which arrays are the best solution.

20 • What is file concatenation? File merging? Give examples.

21 • The text refers to buffer files. Describe a file manipulation problem whose solution relies on the use of a buffer file.

22 • What restrictions does Pascal place on file variables that don't apply to other variable types?

Write a program that ...

23 • Write a program that copies one file to another (every other character, every other line, etc.).

24 • Write a program that merges two textfiles, line by line (character by character, word by word).

25 • Write a program that selectively merges two textfiles (choosing lines that begin with capital letters).

26 • Write a program that reads from input to create a new file, but inserts two blank lines between every line.

27 • Write a program that inspects two textfiles, then adds the longer file to the end of the shorter one.

28 • Write a program that is given a file of numbers (an *integer* file) and prints only the values that are less than the average of the entire file.

29 • A student is taking notes (by computer) in a very bad lecture. Every now and then, the teacher announces that everything she has said so far was wrong, and should be ignored. The student (whose computer has limited memory) wants to tell her program to ignore previous input simply by typing a blank line. Write a program that she can use. It should read input, but ignore everything entered before a blank line. Naturally, it should print everything entered after the last blank line. Do not store any more information than necessary.

30 • Suppose we are given two textfiles. Files A and B have the same number of lines, but every line in file B is at least as long as the corresponding line in file A. Write a program that prints the 'excess' portion of each line in file B (permanently removes the 'excess' from each line of file B).

31 • A program is given two textfiles. Many of the lines in each file match for the first few characters, then are different. Write a program that prints the identical portions (the different portions) of each line.

32 • Suppose we have a textfile, of unknown length, that consists only of words that start with lower-case letters. A single space separates each word. Write a program that prints, in order, every word that starts with 'a', with 'b', and so on. Words beginning with a particular letter do not have to be sorted—just print all the 'a' words, then the 'b' words, etc.

Chapter Fourteen

Understanding code ...

1 • Which of these set expressions represent the same value? [a,b,d,f]

     a) [1..10]   b) [1..5, 6..9, 10]   c) [1..3, ´4´, 5..10]

     d) [1..5, 5, 6..10]   e) [10..6, 5..1]   f) [10, 9, 8, 7, 6, 5, 4, 3, 2, 1]

2 • Which of these set expressions are equivalent? [abcd]

     a) [´A´..´H´]   b) [´A´..´C´] + [´B´..´H´]

     c) [´A´..´K´] − [´I´..´K´]   d) [´A´..´H´] * [´A´..´Z´]

     e) [´A´..´Z´] − [´A´..´H´]

3 • Evaluate these boolean-valued set expressions.

     a)   [´a´..´c´] <= [´b´..´d´]

     b)   [´h´, ´i´, ´j´] in [´h´..´k´]

     c)   [´A´] < [´A´, ´a´]

     d)   [´M´..´Z´] >= [´m´..´z´]

     e)   [´a´, ´b´, ´c´, ´d´, ´e´] <= [´a´..´h´]

     f)   [´M´, ´H´, ´K´] = [´K´, ´H´, ´M´]

     g)   ´.´ in [´.´, ´ ´, ´,´, ´;´]

4 • What are the possible values of *AnimalHouse*? Assume these definitions:

```
type Greeks = (Alpha, Chi, Omega);
var AnimalHouse:  set of Greeks;
```

5 • Suppose that we have made these definitions:

```
type Letters = (Alpha, Beta, Gamma, Delta, Chi, Omega);
     Greek = set of Letters;
var Frat, Sorority:  Greek;
```

What are the values of *Frat* and *Sorority* after each assignment? Assume that the assignments follow each other, as shown.

     a)   Frat := [Alpha..Omega];

     b)   Sorority := Frat − [ ];

     c)   Frat := Frat * Sorority;

                [both are Alpha..Omega]

     d)   Sorority := Sorority − Fraternity + [Beta..Chi];

                [Sorority is Beta..Chi]

     e)   Sorority := ([Beta..Gamma]+Delta)*Frat;

                [Sorority is Beta..Delta]

6 • Find the bug. **[Consonants isn't initialized]**

```
program ConsonantCount (input, output);
{Counts lower-case consonants in input.}
type Lower = ´a´..´z´;
     Holder = set of Lower;
var Consonants:  Holder;
    Count:  integer;
    Ch:  char;
begin
  Count := 0;
  Consonants := Consonants − [´a´, ´e´, ´i´, ´o´, ´u´]; {remove the vowels}
  while not eof do begin
     read (Ch);
     if Ch in Consonants then Count := Count + 1
  end;
  writeln (´There were ´, Count, ´consonants. ´)
end.
```

7 • Assume that we make these assignments, using the types defined above:

```
type Letters = (Alpha, Beta, Gamma, Delta, Chi, Omega);
Frat := [Alpha, Gamma, Chi];
Sorority := [Alpha..Gamma, Chi..Omega];
```

Evaluate these expressions:

a) Frat = Sorority [**false**]
b) Frat < = Sorority [**true**]
c) Sorority > = Frat [**true**]
d) Sorority < = [Alpha, Chi, Omega] [**false**]
e) Frat < > (Frat * Sorority) [**false**]

8 • Describe, in words, what procedure *Test* finds out. Assume that *SomeSetType* has been defined as being of **set of** *char*. [**finds lowest capital letter in Exam.**]

```
procedure Test (Exam: SomeSetType);
   var Temp, Save: char;
   begin
     Save := ' ';
     for Temp := 'Z' to 'A' do
         if Temp in Exam then
             Save := Temp;
      writeln (Save)
   end;
```

9 • What does procedure Test find out? [**the number of values common to F, S, and T**]

```
type Int = 1..128;
     Small = set of Int;

procedure Test (F, S, T: Small);
   var Local: Small;
       i, Count: integer;
   begin
     Count := 0;
     if F < = S then Local := F * T
       else if T < = F then Local := T * S
          else if S < = F then Local := S * T
             else if F < = T then Local := F * S
                else if T < = S then Local := T * F
                   else Local := F * S * T;
     for i := 1 to 128 do
        if i in Local then
            Count := Count + 1;
      writeln (Count)
   end;
```

10 • Here's the input:

This is a test of the emergency broadcast system.

What's the output? Show blanks with underlines. Assume that *Seen* belongs to a **set of** *char* type. [**is_t_he_eroacst_ysem**]

```
Seen := [ ];
while not eof do begin
   read (Ch);
   if Ch in Seen
     then begin
         write (Ch);
         Seen := Seen − [Ch]
     end
     else Seen := Seen + [Ch]
end;
writeln;
```

11 • Here's the input:

> who put the bop in the wop bop a loo bop?

What's the output? Show a space as an underline. [**hp_hb__hw_b_lb?**] (Can be made into 'what's the input?' by, say, reversing the ordering of consonant – vowel pairs.)

```
program BeBop (input, output);
type Letters:  set of char;
var Ch1, Ch2:  char;
    Vowels, Consonants:  Letters;
begin
    Vowels := ['a', 'e', 'i', 'o', 'u'];
    Consonants := ['b'..'z'] — Vowels;
    while not eof do begin
        read (Ch1);
        if Ch1 in Consonants then begin
            read (Ch2);
            if Ch2 in Vowels
                then write (Ch1)
                else write (Ch2)
        end
    end;
    writeln
end.
```

Short responses ...

12 • What is a set's base type? Give an example.

13 • What is a set's cardinality? When is maximum set cardinality an issue for the programmer?

14 • What problems might this definition cause?

> type Numbers = set of integer;

15 • What is a set union? Set difference? Set intersection? Give examples.

Write a program that ...

16 • Write a subprogram that counts the number of times characters in a given set occur in input.

17 • Write a program that counts (vowels, punctuation, digits, non-letters, non-vowels).

18 • Write a program that finds digits that never appear in numerical input, and prints their sum.

19 • Write a subprogram that finds the least and greatest *char* values in a variable of type **set of** *char*.

20 • Write a program that prints the category (upper-case letter, punctuation mark, etc.) of input characterrs.

21 • Write a program that prints letters that have (have not) been duplicated in input.

Chapter Fifteen

Understanding code ...

1 • Assume the definitions and declarations shown below. Which of these calls to procedure *new* are legal? [**b, h, i**]

```
type LinkPointer  =  ↑ Link;
     Link  =  record
                  Data:  integer;
                  Next:  LinkPointer
              end;
var Ptr:  LinkPointer;
    Node:  Link;
```

```
a)    new (Link);
b)    new (Ptr);
c)    new (LinkPointer);
d)    new (Node);
e)    new (Next);
f)    new (Link.Next);
g)    new (Ptr ↑ );
h)    new (Node.Next);
i)    new (Ptr ↑ .Next);
j)    new (Ptr ↑ .Link);
```

2 • Assume the definitions and declarations given above. Which of these statements are legal? Assume that procedure *new* has been called when necessary. [**a−f**]

```
a)    Node.Next := nil;
b)    Ptr := nil;
c)    Ptr ↑ .Next := Ptr;
d)    writeln (Ptr ↑ .Data);
e)    readln (Node.Data);
f)    Ptr ↑  := Node;
g)    Node ↑ .Next := nil;
h)    Node := nil;
i)    Ptr := Node ↑ ;
j)    writeln (Ptr ↑ .Next);
```

For the next three questions, assume that the following linked list has been created:

> (Insert a copy of the linked list from page 481 here)
> (NOTE: a small change is necessary--the last arrow should point to
> **nil** rather than 'undefined'. This is VERY important)

3 • Assume that *Current* and *FirstElement* are pointer variables of the same type. Draw links that show the status of the list after this code segment. Be sure to include any new pointers.

```
Current := FirstElement;
while Current ↑ .Next < > nil do
    Current := Current ↑ .Next;
Current ↑ .Next := FirstElement;
```

4 • Do the same for this code segment. *Temp* is a pointer variable of the same type as *FirstElement*.

```
Current := FirstElement;
while Current < > nil do begin
    Temp := Current;
    Current := Current ↑ .Next;
    Temp ↑ .Next := FirstElement
end;
```

5 • Do the same for this code segment.

```
Current := FirstElement;
Temp := FirstElement;
FirstElement := FirstElement ↑ .Next;
while Temp ↑ .Next < > nil do
    Temp := Temp ↑ .Next;
Temp ↑ .Next := Current;
Current ↑ .Next := nil;
```

For the next four questions, a diagram similar to the one above should be supplied. However, all *Data* fields should actually contain numerical values. For these questions, assume that the values are 1, 2, 3, and 4, respectively.

6 • Assume that the call *PrintList* (*FirstElement*) is made. What is its output? [4 3 2 1]

```
procedure PrintList (Current:ListPointer);
  begin
    if Current ↑ .Next < > nil then
      PrintList (Current ↑ .Next);
    writeln (Current ↑ .Data)
  end;
```

7 • Assume that the call *ShowSome* (*FirstElement*) is made. What is its output? [4]

```
procedure ShowSome (Current:ListPointer);
  begin
    if Current ↑ .Next < > nil
      then ShowSome (Current ↑ .Next)
      else writeln (Current ↑ .Data)
  end;
```

8 • Assume that the call *ShowAll* (*FirstElement*) is made. What is its output? [1 2 3 4]

```
procedure ShowAll (Current: ListPointer);
  begin
    writeln (Current ↑ .Data);
    if Current ↑ .Next < > nil then
      ShowAll (Current ↑ .Next)
  end;
```

9 • Assume that the call *PrintSomething* (*FirstElement*) is made. What is its output? [4 4 4 4]

```
procedure PrintSomething (var Current: ListPointer);
  begin
    if Current ↑ .Next < > nil then begin
      Current := Current ↑ .Next;
      PrintSomething (Current)
    end;
    writeln (Current ↑ .Data)
  end;
```

The next six questions refer to a binary tree that has been initialized as:

Its elements are defined as:

```
type NodePointer = ↑ Node;
     Node = record
                Data: integer;
                Lower, Higher: NodePointer
            end;
```

10 • What is the output of the call *PrintTree* (*Root*)? Assume that *Root* references the root of the tree. [**2 3 4 5 7 9**]

```
procedure PrintTree (Current: NodePointer);
   begin
      if Current↑.Lower <> nil then
         PrintTree (Current↑.Lower);
      write (Current↑.Data);
      if Current↑.Higher <> nil then
         PrintTree (Current↑.Higher)
   end;
```

11 • What is the output of the call *Leafy* (*Root*)? Assume that *Root* references the root of the tree. [**9 7 5 4 3 2**]

```
procedure Leafy (Current: NodePointer);
   begin
      if Current↑.Higher <> nil then
         Leafy (Current↑.Higher);
      write (Current↑.Data);
      if Current↑.Lower <> nil then
         Leafy (Current↑.Lower)
   end;
```

12 • What is the output of the call *Woody* (*Root*)? Assume that *Root* references the root of the tree. [**2 2 4 4 7 9 9**]

```
procedure Woody (Current: NodePointer);
   begin
      if Current↑.Lower <> nil
         then Woody (Current↑.Lower)
         else write (Current↑.Data);
      if Current↑.Higher <> nil
         then Woody (Current↑.Higher)
         else write (Current↑.Data)
   end;
```

13 • What is the output of the call *NutTree* (*Root*)? Assume that *Root* references the root of the tree. [**5 3 2 4 7 9**]

```
procedure NutTree (Current: NodePointer);
   begin
      write (Current↑.Data);
      if Current↑.Lower <> nil then
         NutTree (Current↑.Lower);
      if Current↑.Higher <> nil then
         NutTree (Current↑.Higher)
   end;
```

14 • What is the output of the call *FruitTree* (*Root*)? Assume that *Root* references the root of the tree. [**2**]

```
procedure FruitTree (Current: NodePointer);
   begin
      if Current↑.Lower <> nil
         then FruitTree (Current↑.Lower)
         else if Current↑.Higher <> nil
            then FruitTree (Current↑.Higher)
            else write (Current↑.Data)
   end;
```

15 • What is the output of the call *FindNodes* (*Root*)? Assume that *Root* references the root of the tree. [**2 2 4 4 7 9 9**]

```
procedure FindNodes (Current: NodePointer);
   begin
      if Current ↑ .Lower = nil
         then write (Current ↑ .Data)
         else FindNodes (Current ↑ .Lower);
      if Current ↑ .Higher = nil
         then write (Current ↑ .Data)
         else FindNodes (Current ↑ .Higher)
   end;
```

Short responses ...

16 • How can a pointer be given a value? What are legal pointer values?

17 • What is the difference between a **nil** pointer, and one that is uninitialized?

18 • What is an address? How does it relate to the value of a pointer?

19 • Suppose that a variable named *Pointer* belongs to a pointer type. Can *Pointer* (not a field of *Pointer*) ever be used in an output statement? In an **if** statement?

20 • Suppose that *High, Low*, and *Middle* have been defined like this:

```
type IntPoint = ↑ integer;
var High, Low, Middle: IntPoint;
```

What is wrong with each of these statements? How would you correct them?

```
Low := 7;
High ↑ := nil;
Middle := Low + High;
writeln (Low);
```

21 • What is an auxiliary pointer? Give examples of situations in which such pointers are useful.

22 • Suppose that these type definitions are available to us:

```
type Line = array [1..80] of char;
     Page = array [1..1000] of Line;
     LinePointer = ↑ Line;
     PointPage = record
                     Current: Line;
                     Next: LinePointer
                  end;
```

Under what circumstances might we prefer to use type *Page* over type *PointPage*? Give applications for which each type is the best solution.

23 • Are data structures constructed with pointers random access or sequential access? Can you give examples that weaken an argument for one or the other?

Write a program that ...

For these questions, it's a good idea to provide the definition of a standard element:

```
type LinkPointer = ↑ Link;
     Link = record
                Data: DataType;
                Next: LinkPointer
             end;
```

```
type DoublePointer = ↑ DoubleLink;
     DoubleLink = record
                      Data: DataType;
                      Next, Previous: DoubleLink
                   end;
```

```
type NodePointer  =  ↑ Node;
      Node  = record
                  Data:  DataType;
                  Left, Right:  Node
              end;
```

24 • Write a subprogram that prints the contents of a linked list.

25 • Write a subprogram that, using recursion, prints a linked list in reverse.

26 • Write a subprogram that advances a pointer to the end of a linked list.

27 • Write a subprogram that reverses the contents of a linked list with (without) recursion.

28 • Write a subprogram that joins two lists.

29 • Write a subprogram that inserts an element after (before) the current (the first) (the nth) element in a list.

30 • Write a subprogram that reverses the elements of a doubly-linked list without using recursion.

31 • Write a subprogram that transfers the elements of a singly-linked list to a doubly-linked list.

32 • Write a subprogram that counts the elements of a list (nodes of a tree).

33 • Write a subprogram that removes the first (next) n elements from a linked list.

34 • Write a subprogram that reinserts element m after postion n in a linked list.

35 • Write a subprogram that is given a pointer to the root of an alphabetically ordered binary tree, and prints its nodes' data in alphabetical order (in reverse order).

36 • Write a subprogram that is given a pointer to the root of an alphabetically ordered binary tree, and transfers its contents, in order, to a linked list.

37 • Write procedures *Save* and *Retrieve* that maintain a FIFO list (a LIFO list).

38 • Write procedures that add and retrieve elements from a deque. One argument supplied to the procedures will indicate the proper end of the deque.

A Note on the Staff Meetings

This section contains a collection of brief discussions regarding, and handouts for, staff meetings. It is essentially the curriculum of *Teaching Practice* 300; a course that I give in conjunction with my Pascal class.

At Berkeley, 300-series courses are a special category of 'hands-on practice' classes, offered by many departments. A variable number of credits are allowed, and the course may be repeated to some statutory maximum. Students usually sign up for 10 hours per week (3 units, out of a normal load of 15), on a pass/no pass basis. One hour weekly is devoted to class discussion, with the remainder spent in the terminal room.

I think that staff development is an important and entirely worthwhile expenditure of my time. In the short term, my students benefit from staff members who are being encouraged to hone their own teaching skills. In the long run, I'm preparing the 'middle-management' of future staffs; developing reader leaders and head TA's who can make my life easier.

I have included eight weekly packets, in rough order of presentation. They are:

1.   Course principles: establishing the basic attitudes of the staff.
2.   Section Notes, and Consulting/Grading Advice: preparing for the first day on the job.
3.   Developing Explanations: learning the difference between advice, and good advice.
4.   Grading Practice: suggestions for making grading low-key and effective.
5.   Grading Criteria: developing judgement for subjective grading decisions.
6.   Asking Questions: handling questions and discussion in section.
7.   Crisis!: dealing with crises that develop in the terminal room.
8.   Staff Responsibilities: encouraging the staff to make each other's lives easier.

The material supplied here occupies about half of our weekly meeting time, with the rest devoted to dealing with problems, assessing the current state of the course, and discussing details related to the current assignment. In most cases, discussion of particular points actually takes more than one week; hence the rather short schedule of handouts.

Some topics I haven't prepared handouts for, but always end up discussing, are preparing exams, grading and assigning final grades, selecting a rounded staff, and other points of interest to any instructor. I would appreciate very much the opportunity to see any handouts you find useful in dealing with your own staff, possibly for inclusion in the next edition of this manual.

Staff Meeting 1

Introduction

The first week's staff meeting is invariably a madhouse because *a*) TA's haven't been contacted by the graduate office; *b*) you still haven't gotten all the reader applications; *c*) your budget for both are being cut anyway; and *d*) more and more total randoms keep showing up to volunteer for credit. Nevertheless, I put together a talk to welcome the troops. I have two intentions:

- I want to say hello, and to get people excited.

If I want a challenging curriculum that can be successfully completed by most students, I need to have an enthusiastic staff. My experience is that the amount of material I can put into my course depends mainly on the staff's strength. Since staff members are not usually closely supervised or evaluated during the term, the staff meeting is the best chance I have to motivate them.

- I want to make sure that we all have the same idea about overall course aims.

My objective is to teach the most computer science to the most students. Other *possible* goals might be weeding out weaker students, spotting and encouraging the strongest students, keeping the terminal room quiet, etc. However, these are not *my* goals. I encourage the staff to think of themselves as teachers, rather than as monitors.

Strawbosses

I try to keep a terminal room staffed up to twelve hours a day, seven days a week. To schedule 9 hour-a-week staff members, I appoint a temporary 'strawboss' (who has prior staff experience) for each day, and divide the week into three groups of 2−3 days. Then, each staff member is required to sign up for a 3-hour slot in two groups. Finally, the strawbosses caucus, and fill out remaining openings through a combination of plea and threat.

The strawboss system allows flexibility in the early parts of the term when staff members aren't sure of their schedules. Each strawboss has to keep the terminal room running for 'her' day, and should keep an eye on it by calling up or dropping in occasionally. The strawboss makes sure that new staff know what to do, and reassigns or covers open hours.

Handouts

Two handouts are shown opposite: the volunteer staff recruitment flyer, and the course principles memo. The recruitment flyer goes up the week before classes start. I usually discuss the principles memo, point-by-point, in the first meeting or two.

Doug Cooper and Computer Science 8 Invite You To

Consult for Credit!

Course: Computer Science 300 — Teaching Experience

Units: 1−3, P/NP. 3 units require 9 hours of consulting per week.

Duties: Terminal room consulting and face-to-face grading of hordes of CS 8 (Introduction to Pascal) students.

Prerequisites: Excellent performance in the first CS Major course, patience, good humor.

Benefits:

- THRILL! to the happy sight of a terminal room full of confused programmers, whose problems only *you* can solve;
- FIND OUT! why consultants have such a good time that they end up hanging out in the terminal room even when they're not working;
- GET! something to put on your resume or CS major application;
- PAY BACK! the students who volunteered to help when you were young and ignorant.
- MEET! hundreds of students to whom *you* will be a true Programming God;
- HELP! make CS 8 work in the face of total understaffing and lack of equipment.

Not to mention cementing your own knowledge of Pascal, becoming more comfortable in dealing with people, learning quite a bit about how to teach and encourage students, vastly improving your chances of getting a paid job in the future, and getting a behind-the-scenes view of how a large CS class is run.

Contact: dbcooper@arpa (473 Evans, 642-4951)
            spirakis@ingres

I particularly encourage women and students whose first language is not English to apply.

Organizational meeting: Monday Aug. 26, 4 P.M. in 60 Evans. This will be the staff meeting time for the rest of the term.

Please try to attend the first lecture (Monday 11-12 in 145 Dwinelle). You will not have to attend class in the future.

Doug Cooper   Course Principles   Introductory Pascal

I like to run my course according to the following principles. Please read them, and bring up any questions you may have at the next staff meeting.

Students have a right to be taught.

It's not enough to present the facts, and expect the students to be motivated enough to figure them out by themselves. Let's not just lecture—let's *teach* instead.

Poor students have the same right to an education as good ones.

Let's not let anybody fall by the wayside. Although it may be most gratifying to help sharp students, they need us the least. Seek out students who are doing poorly, or who are shy, or who are afraid to ask questions. Every student has earned his or her place at Berkeley—make that mean something more than a seat.

The staff represents the University.

Whether or not we consider what we're doing to be just a job, we represent the University to our students. Try to measure your conduct toward them in this light. Each one of us has the power to make education either pleasant or miserable for the student.

The customer is usually right—try to never argue.

Most arguments have nothing to do with the point under debate. Even if you are right, arguing with students demeans both of you. Try to change the student's attitude toward the issue or its importance, rather than her stand on the issue itself.

Students have problems of their own.

Remember that our students are very young; many are immigrants, or have family problems, or are simply not prepared for the pressure of Berkeley. Unfortunately, undergraduates get little formal social or emotional support from the University. Try to recall this when their actions or attitudes start to drive you crazy.

Staff Meeting 2

Role Playing

The first staff meeting was mainly announcements, but subsequent meetings are usually devoted to discussion. On a superficial level, I want to make sure that the staff hears (or tells me) about any problems that have come up, and that they have read and understood the handouts. As a deeper goal, I want to help them develop the ability to 'do the right thing' when a supervisor isn't around. In my mind, staff discussions are just as necessary as class lectures, and their content and purpose has to be considered just as carefully.

Role playing is the best technique I've found for provoking fruitful staff discussions. In a direct form, staff members take the part of students or staff associated with the course, and respond to problems raised by me or other players. The direct approach is particularly good when I'm trying to develop uniform responses; as when I want to make sure that staff will have a single voice in regard to grading. I throw out the characteristics of a student's homework, and the staff member describes her evaluation of it out loud.

Direct role playing is effective when we're dealing with a clear agenda. I find that a reverse sort of role playing is useful for helping the staff learn about hidden agendas. Instead of having the staff play at being 'good' students and helpers, I encourage them to be obnoxious, unruly, and unhelpful. I think this approach helps staff develop a subtler appreciation of the attitudes and statements that cause problems.

Handouts

The first attached handout, titled *Section Notes*, is for the graduate student TA staff. It summarizes the differences between the Lecture Review and Problem Solving sections, and gives some tips for preparation.

The second handout, titled *Consulting/Grading Advice*, is aimed more at the reading and consulting staff. Its tone is quite different—this handout is intended for sophomores with little or no teaching experience.

Doug Cooper   Section Notes   Introductory Pascal

Section Type and Content

Weekly section meetings are divided into two types. *Lecture review* sections should deal with material that was introduced in class, or which has to do with the homework. There should be a lot of questions and student/TA interaction in these sections. Typical coverage might include a reprise of some hard lecture material, some random questions about the computer and its operating system, homework problems or suggestions, and some small explanatory programs.

Problem solving sections, in contrast, should deal with problem solving in general. For our course, problem solving will usually mean learning how to go from problem statement to Pascal code. The problems themselves won't require many clever algorithms or tricks. Instead, the student's difficulty will consistently lie in understanding the problem, doing problem decomposition or stepwise refinement, and writing pseudocode.

Please read over the Xeroxed pages from Oh! Pascal! Exercises marked 'R' should be used as an outline for topics in the Lecture Review sections. You can refer to, and solve, the problems, or can use them as illustrative answers for questions. Be sure to look them all over. Sometimes discussion can get sidetracked, and a lot of details left out. Gauge your time left as you go along, and refer people to office or consultant hours if they're really confused, or if they want to discuss much harder problems.

The exercises marked 'P' are for the Problem Solving sections. There are too many problems to do, but try to hit 4 to 6. If people have VERY short random questions, answer them, but refer longer questions to the other sections or office hours to avoid getting sidetracked.

Remember that students are often confused when they read English language problem statements. The purpose of these sections is to show straightforward methods of jumping into programs. Be sure to remind students that if they get lost in one problem, a new one will be along in a few minutes. In general, I usually:

1.   Decompose the problem into its main parts.
2.   Write some trial code on scratch paper to take care of the central 'calculation' or I/O.
3.   Write a pseudocode outline.

You'll see that some of the programs are too long to do in 5−10 minutes. Do a rough draft: just enough to make the final program obvious.

To Be Prepared...

For lecture review sections, review notes of the week's lectures (either Black Lightning or student notes will be fine). Skim the reading and assignment. Outline your talk with a brief list of topics—the first set of short exercises at the end of the chapter usually illustrates most of the points that may confuse students. If you have trouble thinking on your feet (like me!), write the code of some of the marked exercises.

For problem solving sections, read the marked problems carefully. For each you choose, write a brief note on a first-level decomposition, a high-point of the program, and a rough pseudo-code. Try putting some 'timing marks' in your notes to make sure that you don't get hung up on one particular problem.

Doug Cooper   Consulting/Grading Advice   Introductory Pascal

Consulting

Most terminal room work falls under the heading of consulting. This includes:

1. Helping with *system mechanics*, including terminals, printers, and UNIX system details.
2. Helping with the *course*; explaining requirements, due dates, etc.
3. Helping with *homework*, which generally includes assistance with Pascal and algorithm details.
4. Helping with *morale*, which may involve putting students at ease, introducing them to each other, and making coffee.

Questions

• Imagine a problem that might arise under each of these headings. How would you deal with it?

• Imagine yourself as a very bad consultant. How would you deal with things differently?

• What goes into making consulting satisfying for the consultant? How does a 'bad' student make consulting less satisfying?

• What goes into making study in the terminal room satisfying for the student? How does a 'bad' consultant make studying less satisfying?

Grading

Grading for the first few weeks is Pass/No Pass. Why?

1. P/NP grading reduces tension in the terminal room, and makes the course more fun for students.
2. It encourages students to ask for help, and lets the consultants give it. It starts the student/grader relationship on the right foot.
3. It helps guarantee that the student will master basic material.
4. It lets graders learn how to grade, and students learn how to be graded.

Many of you went through this grading process when you were my students. What are the main features of face-to-face grading?

• Take the first 15 − 30 seconds to say hi to the student, and have her say hi to you. Establish that you're both people working under constraints.

• Testing skills (like editing or UNIX) is best handled through selective sampling. Naturally you don't have to ask every question. Instead, try to ask some representative questions that are different from the ones given in the assignment.

• Testing and reading programs, at this point, is mainly an opportunity to congratulate and point out alternatives. A student might not have indented—point out what the indented version looks like. A program might work perfectly—point out another approach that also works.

• If a student doesn't seem to have mastered the material, send her back to the terminal for some more practice. If she is having a great deal of difficulty, or if a deadline is near, have her work with another student who's doing better.

Questions

• How long does it take a student to master Vi? To write her first program? Do you remember what your very first program felt like?

• What does the student expect to get from the grader? What does the grader expect to get from the student? If everybody passes, should P/NP grades be recorded? How?

• What are some wrong things to say when you're grading an ordinary program? An outstanding one? A poor one? What are some wrong things that a student might say to you?

• Be a brand new grader—what do you want an experienced grader to tell you? Be an experienced grader—what are the most important things to say to a novice?

Staff Meeting 3

Frameworks and Paradigms

My discussion topics for this meeting are the *frameworks* we use to classify knowledge, and the *paradigms* we should present to help students build their own frameworks. I'm not using these terms as the basis of any formal theory of learning. However, I do think we can agree that it's easier to learn once one has a conceptual model—a framework with open slots for new facts—of the topic at hand.

For example, I've found that students have trouble with their first text editor because they barely understand what an editor is supposed to do. The second one is easier because they have a framework to go by; they know that an editor will include commands for searching, appending, deletion, and the like. Programming languages can follow a like pattern; as do particular classes of algorithms, etc.

From the staff's point of view, helping students build frameworks means that the examples they use to answer questions have to be more than simple explanations. They should be paradigms that help strengthen the students' framework of understanding. Most important, the staff should be aware that, on occasion, a straightforward example or explanation should be avoided if it introduces a new set of paradigms that can confuse the student.

For instance, I teach my students a subset of editor commands that allow a simple framework: commands begin in a certain way, end in a certain way, etc. There may, on occasion, be editor commands that require fewer keystrokes than the ones I teach. However, I avoid them because they require a more complicated framework: another form of command. I caution my staff to introduce new commands in a way that fits the existing patterns. The simpler command may save a bit now, but it makes it harder for the student to develop general rules.

Now, as teachers, we have experience in choosing examples, explanations, and even words carefully; not necessarily because they're best for *today's* lecture, but because they will fit in properly with lessons given later in the term. Staff members tend not to have this prescience, though, partly because they haven't thought about how students internalize knowledge, and partly because they take a very short-term view of the course. My goal this week is to encourage staff members to take a longer view in developing explanations that are consistent and clear.

Handout

The *Developing Explanations* handout, attached, is a guide for a discussion of explanations. I use it to help staff distinguish the relative value of different approaches to helping students. I try to stress the idea that students may require different kinds of explanations, and that different explanations can be equally 'simple' or 'crystal clear.'

As is often the case, role playing is extremely helpful in making staff aware of the problems they'll be facing. In my experience, explanations of *read* and *readln*, or of the declaration and use of parameters, provide particularly good examples for discussion.

Doug Cooper   Developing Explanations   Introductory Pascal

What makes some people good at explaining things? Is it enough to invent a slow, clear explanation? Or will a good explainer's examples vary from student to student? As a student, have you ever been given an explanation that just confused you? As a consultant, have you ever felt that you were 'undoing' a previous consultant's poor explanation?

Being able to deliver a successful explanation to a confused student is one of the most rewarding aspects of teaching. How can you improve your own ability to explain things? Here are some suggestions:

• **Make a chart.** Graphically represent this week's topics in relation to topics from the prior or subsequent week. Which branch of the 'statement category' tree are we on this week? How has what the student learned in the current week changed her picture of Pascal? What hints can we drop that will lead into next week?

• **Consider alternatives.** Think of two or three ways to answer a question. Do explanations ever lead to conclusions? How can a correct explanation lead to an incorrect conclusion? What about the reverse? Can a good explanation of how to get the job done be a bad paradigm?

• **Classify.** Associate a name with your answer or suggestion, e.g. the 'many variable approach,' or the 'use the same pair over again' method. Can you imagine referring back to the same name next week?

• **Limit vocabulary.** Consciously limit your 'explanation vocabulary' to terms or commands that you know students know (e.g. have appeared on editor command summary lists).

• **Distort explanations.** Suppose that we were to teach Pascal using recursion for the simplest iteration. How might that change an explanation this week? Suppose that all variables (even simple variables) were accessed through pointers. What then?

• **Change ground levels.** Obviously we'd give different sorts of explanations to a novice programmer, and one who already knows several programming languages. Think of your explanation to an expert—what framework does it rely on? Now consider why you can't give the same explanation to a novice—what frameworks are they missing?

• **Listen to terms.** Listen to the words and phrases that students use to describe their problems. Are students having difficulty simply because they're not formulating questions precisely? Are they able to distinguish between programs (say, the editor and the shell), or are they confusing different aspects of 'the system?' Can restating the question provide an answer?

Staff Meeting 4

Grading Practice

In my course, the fourth week's assignment is given a point grade that is not recorded. This exercise serves several purposes:

1. Staff must learn the criteria used for grading. They have to learn what points I consider to be important, and what the relative weight of program features are.

2. Students also have to learn what grading criteria are. They tend to be overly concerned with the 'right answer,' or with program efficiency, and must be taught that less urgent features (like comments) are likely to be weighted heavily in grading.

3. Staff must learn how to grade, and students have to learn how to be graded. They must both learn to distinguish between grading the program, and judging the programmer.

4. A trial grading run is useful in developing consistency among the staff. It also gives students a taste of the wait they are liable to encounter when they wait until the last minute to log in.

In my experience, making grading be a positive experience for student and staffer alike is a crucial element of a successful course. I believe that students will work much harder to earn the approval of an appreciative staff member than they will to garner criticism of their efforts. Similarly, staff consistently point to the pressure of grading hostile students as one of the least attractive features of working for a programming course.

I have usually found that one can get a good sense of the relative value of a program without much effort. Generally, student programs fall into three groups—great, all right, and awful. In staff meetings, we will often discuss the characteristics of programs in these three groups; e.g. a program with poor comments can never be great, a program without procedures or parameters must be awful, a great program can still have a bug in one feature, etc. My experience is that although different staffers may point to different particular features in distinguishing a good program from a great one, they will invariably agree on the gross classification.

I think that point-by-point checklists are bad for two reasons. First, I find it's harder to ensure consistency; two programs may be obviously 'all right,' yet garner different point totals from one reader to the next. Second, I think that checklists make grading too judgemental; the student is the passive recipient of a rating, instead of being an involved partner in a consultation.

As a result, I encourage my staff to try to form their opinion of a program before they open their mouths, then use grading to justify this opinion to the student. We say 'I think the program is just average, and here's why,' instead of 'I've taken off for this, this, and this, and that (according to my chart) makes your program average.'

I strongly encourage the staff to look for something positive in every program 'This procedure is really good,' 'I really like your comments,' 'your indenting makes your program much easier to read.'

(continued)

Handout

The attached handout lays out a mental checklist for the grading session—not of points to take off for, but of attitudes and approaches I'd like the staff to bear in mind. Reverse role playing (trying to *ignore* every suggestion) is handy. As mentioned above, I stress the point that when students don't panic at grading time, the job of consulting is much more fun.

Doug Cooper   Grading   Introductory Pascal

Before you sit down...

1.   Take a moment to be a person, not a grading machine.

If the student thinks that you're a machine, she'll treat you like one—badly. When you first sit down, take 15−30 seconds to find out the student's name, and to tell her yours.

2.   No matter how awful the student's program is, it is a program that she has worked long and hard on.

Statistics generally show that the poorest students spend the most time working on their programs. Appreciate the student's effort, even if it isn't paying off for her yet. 'It looks like you put a lot of work into this.' is a good way to acknowledge her effort.

3.   Recognize that the most satisfaction comes from a successful program.

Poor programmers get the least inherent reward from their work. They need the most encouragement to go back and try to do better on the next assignment. Students who are doing badly are least likely to be enthusiastic on their own.

Discussing the program

1.   Grade the program, not the student.

Always, *always* refer to 'the program,' rather than to 'your program.' Avoid putting the student on the defensive—a student who is busy defending her work isn't listening to suggestions for improvement next time.

2.   Talk to the student, not the program.

A program does not necessarily reflect the student's current understanding—her mistakes may have made her smarter than her program indicates. We've all had the experience of finishing a large program, and saying to ourselves 'Gee, if I had to do that over again, I'd...' Give the programmer a chance to tell you what she knows now. Remember that the purpose of face-to-face grading is to help the student master the assignment. If we just wanted to calculate a grade, her presence wouldn't be necessary.

3.   Spot the good points.

Every program, no matter how atrocious it is, has something good about it. You *must* find a program feature worthy of congratulation. It is particularly effective to mention it in a manner that offsets some problem: 'The identifiers weren't very good, but your comments were so great that I won't count off for them this time.'

Assigning the grade.

1.   Make criticism effective.

A recounting of a program's shortcomings is only effective if the list is short. Remember that students most likely to get a long list of problems will probably be least able to deal with them. Try to focus on the student's main problems, without overwhelming her: 'There are some problems with layout, but I think you should concentrate on...'

2.   Give the student a goal.

One reason students write poor programs is that they're not skilled at distinguishing important features. Give the student reasonable goals for her next program: 'Get a simple version working first,' 'be sure that you use both kinds of parameters.' Try to establish a personal connection with the student: 'For next week, I'd like to see...'

Staff Meeting 5

Grading criteria

My first step in preparing the staff to grade programs is to explain what I'm looking for. My programming assignments rarely require the discovery of particularly difficult answers, so simply checking the output is not enough. Instead, I try to get my staff to treat programs rather like English papers. I stress the idea that, in evaluating programs, method is as important as conclusion.

I take two tacks in helping my readers, who are barely past introductory Pascal themselves, learn to grade. First I point out the more subtle measures of program goodness. Meaningful identifiers, comments, use of procedures, and the like may not make an immediate contribution to program success, but they're important in the long run. Just as an English professor insists on reasonable sentence and paragraph structure even in short papers, I insist that the basic tools of program clarity always be employed.

My second aim is to sensitize my readers to the intention behind assignments. Am I looking for some particular answer, or for a certain method? Does the assignment have anything to do with the lecture, or the reading? How does it relate to the previous assignment, or to the next one? It is hard for me to remember to anticipate and answer all these questions at weekly staff meetings, so I try to develop my graders' independent judgement.

Handout

The attached handout is given to both staff and students. In discussing the criteria with the staff, I usually dwell on the more subjective aspects. In particular, I want the staff to learn to recognize the point at which the lesson is getting across to the student. As a trivial example, how many spaces should statements be indented? Zero or one is probably too few, but neurotically counting precisely four or eight spaces probably isn't a good idea either. I want the staff to recognize that consistency and ease of reading is what's important, and that it may take a variety of forms.

A more serious example involves the use of subprograms and parameters. My intention in the first parameter assignment is to have students practice declaring and using value and variable parameters. I want the staff to recognize that practice of this sort is my goal, rather than finding the answer to whatever question I posed in the assignment.

As usual, I find that role playing is a useful technique in stimulating discussion. A quick stop by the terminal room wastebasket, on the way to the staff meeting, provides any necessary props.

Doug Cooper   Homework Grading Outline   Introductory Pascal

This is an outline of the criteria we use for grading programs. All programs are graded on a twenty-point basis. The first few programs are pass-fail, and the rest carry increasing weight.

Homework overall counts for 25% of your grade. However, most people will get high grades on homework. This means that the midterms and final will determine most of your final grade. It also means that *not* doing homework will hurt your grade.

Read this outline of grading criteria carefully. Try to work within our guidelines by understanding that they set a general outline of the characteristics of a good program—not a line-by-line description of indentation or commenting requirements. Put yourself in the position of a reader when you assess your program.

Remember that homework grading is intended to help you write better programs. Readers will point out your program's really good points, as well as areas that they feel are *most* in need of work. Readers won't complain about every last little flaw—they're not out to blast either you or your code.

STYLE

• Indenting and layout. Is the program readable? Does indenting help debugging and reading? Are parts of the program clearly labeled?

• Identifiers. Are identifiers meaningful and mnemonic? Do they describe their purpose?

• Comments. Is the program reasonably commented? Does the commenting help both the programmer and the grader? Could another student in the class figure the program out?

PROGRAM

• Algorithm. Is the program sensible? Does it solve the problem in a reasonable manner?

• Modularity. Does the program take advantage of procedures and functions? Are its separate parts easy to isolate for testing and debugging?

• Working. Does the program work? Does it fulfill the problem description, or does it solve some other problem? Is it written in a way that lets shortcomings be recognized and fixed?

USER INTERFACE

• I/O. Does the program prompt for the input it needs? Does the program's output confuse or enlighten the user? Are the program's results clearly labeled? Does the program explain itself when necessary?

• Robustness. Is the program robust? Is input error-checked? If not, are explicit instructions given to the user (and in comments)?

JUDGEMENT

• Interpretation. Did the programmer show good judgement in deciding exactly what fine (or unclear) points of the problem statement meant?

• Modification. If the program only solves part of the problem, does it best utilize the programmer's time and talents? Can the programmer 'defend' her choices in algorithm, style, and program to the reader?

Staff Meeting 6

Asking Questions

There is a tendency for inexperienced teachers (like teaching assistants) to think that lecturing consists of presenting material, perhaps accompanied by the comment: 'I'm going to talk now, and if you have any questions, let me know.'

The experienced teacher knows better. The instructor has to be able to engage her students' active interest. She may rely on tricks of pacing, presentation, and the like. But most of all, an effective instructor has to know how to ask, and provoke, questions.

Questions are particularly important in sections. I devote at least one staff meeting to helping teaching assistants develop their ability to encourage class discussion. In the staff meeting, I focus on the following points:

- Formulating self-checks: I think that students are often unable to accurately gauge their own understanding. I encourage the staff to phrase questions or pose problems that will help student self-assessment.

- Encouraging thinking: It is hoped that the TA is capable of answering any questions that come up in section. However, I suggest that the TA work at being a discussion leader, rather than an oracle.

- Cultural expectations: Some staff members may not recognize that, in the U.S., active discussion is encouraged in class. Back home, students may be annoyed at being asked to speak up. Here, the opposite is often true—students are annoyed if they don't get the chance to ask questions.

Handout

The attached handout includes specific suggestions for classroom comments. A 'TA Training' course, if your school has one, is a good source of additional material.

Doug Cooper   Asking Questions   Introductory Pascal

Problem Questions

Here are my nominations for the five worst possible questions.

1. Are there any questions?

A sure prescription for total silence. Who wants to be the first to avow ignorance? What if my question is trivial, or isn't relevant? Try to refine the question: 'Are there questions about...?' 'For instance, is anyone having trouble with...?' 'Such and such is a hard topic. Are there any particular points you'd like to go over again?'

2. Who didn't follow that? (Is there anybody who doesn't understand?)

Ditto.

3. Who knows the answer?

Students who have given wrong answers in the past tend to see this kind of question as a setup for humiliation. Instead, phrase the question in a way that recognizes the difficulty of doing a problem: 'Who'd like to try answering this?' 'Does anybody have an idea for how to start on this one?'

4. Do you see why you're wrong?

Avoid personalizing confusion or mistakes. Instead, try 'Can you see why the first approach won't work?', or 'Can you imagine the problem that would lead to?'

5. The run-on question (generic)

After you ask the question, shut up! Don't continue to refine the question, add more parts, restate it, etc. Once is enough; don't elaborate: 'Does anybody see what the bug is...near the loop...that's giving us the off-by-one error...that we noticed in our test data...a semantic error because the program compiled...'

Positive reinforcement

How can we encourage students to continue to speak up? Here are some suggestions for ways to help motivate continued class discussion.

1. Compliment comments

Try 'that's a good answer,' 'that's a good question,' or 'I'm glad you asked that.' Even a totally wrong answer can be turned around: 'Actually, that's a very hard point—I can see why parameters are easy to confuse.'

2. Identify viewpoints

Give credit to individuals who have helped define the discussion: 'As Susie suggested...,' 'but what about Monica's alternative algorithm?'

3. Help everyone get a right answer

Don't throw a struggling student overboard (by moving on to the next hand). Instead, help her out: 'Well, what *first* step might you take?' 'Suppose we simplify the problem like this...' 'Try to describe what you want to do in English, not Pascal' 'Can you remember which lecture example was similar?'

4. Give everyone a chance

After asking a question, try looking at the board or at your desk for fifteen—thirty seconds to give everyone a chance to think about the answer. Don't always pick the first hands, or the same students—give slow or shy students a chance. Sometimes it's a good idea to pick a student directly—she may know the answer, but be too shy to volunteer. However, make sure that you give them an opportunity to pass: 'Jane, how'd you like to try this one?'

Staff Meeting 7

Student Crisis

What do you do when you find a student crying at his or her terminal? My topic for this meeting would be unusual for most courses. However, I've found that the introductory programming course seems to have an unusual impact on students. I think that it's the instructor's responsibility to help her staff deal with problems—crises in the terminal room—that can reasonably be expected to arise in the course of a term.

Why is the first C.S. course so effective at provoking and/or consolidating student anxiety? First of all, it's hard. The subject matter is new, students have almost no base-level computer science expertise, they have poor study habits and even worse programming habits. Given the difficulty that students have with mathematics courses (even after years of practice), it is not surprising that the layers of abstraction that have to be learned almost overnight in the first computer course can form an almost insurmountable barrier to some students. Students are shaken at a very fundamental level—they suddenly meet material that, try as they might, they simply cannot master.

Second, many of the forms that difficulty takes in C.S. are particularly discouraging. It's one thing to have to struggle with honest-to-goodness program bugs, but endlessly correcting typing mistakes reduces the student to ninth-grade hopelessness. Early errors (like accidentally destroyed files) seem to conspire to make the student feel stupid. Problems with the computing environment (like system crashes) that we have learned to take in stride are hard to understand and thoroughly demoralizing.

Third, the student may think that expertise in computer science is necessary for her future. This goes further than simple entry to a major; I routinely see students who have somehow become convinced that lack of computer ability will render them unemployable. In other words, failing some other course might screw up their chances for a particular plan of study, but messing up in computer science will inhibit them in every up and coming field.

Fourth and finally, difficulty is often confronted publicly. Again and again the student discovers her flaws in a terminal room, while surrounded by her classmates, some of whom may be meeting with considerably more success.

Handout

The attached Crisis! handout provides a rough outline for the meeting. Some preamble may be required; I can still remember the reader who timidly raised his hand and asked 'You mean, we're supposed to find out what's wrong?' Having staff members describe their own particularly hopeless programming moments is another good way to get things started ('Have I ever told you how long it took me to get that bowling program in Chapter 6 working...?').

Doug Cooper   Crisis!   Introductory Pascal

The Symptoms
What do students do when they get upset?

- Cry at the terminal.
- Stare at the terminal without moving for a long, long, time. (Warning: This is also a sign of being dead.)
- Yell at the reader.

The Problems
What are some immediate reasons for getting upset?

- Fear that the assignment won't be completed on time.
- Frustration with program bugs, or the system.
- Worry about upcoming tests.
- Worry about passing the course.
- Worry about getting into a desired major.

And to make it worse...
What are some of the things that turn little problems (e.g. the program won't compile) into big problems?

- Trouble with boyfriends or girlfriends.
- Problems, with parents or other family, that may not have anything to do with school.
- Doubts about ability to make it at the college level ('They must have let me in by mistake...').
- Embarrassment at not being able to get over 'dumb' programming errors, and humiliation at having to confront problems publicly, in the terminal room.

Solutions
What can you do to defuse the situation?

- Get the student out of the terminal room immediately. Go out in the hall for a drink of water, ask him or her to get you a Coke from the vending machines, send him or her for a listing, etc.
- Talk about something completely different. Give the student a chance to relax. Tell him or her your own troubles of the day.
- Put the assignment into its proper perspective in relation to the course. Give the student 'permission' to skip some particularly difficult part (i.e. point out that the grade penalty will be small).
- Remind the student that the assignment is just one small part of college, and not a referendum on his or her ability overall.
- Make a new agenda. Give the student a deadline extension, or suggest someone who can help with the assignment, or with the course. Make sure he or she has a plan for the next few days.
- Set up a longer-term personal connection. Ask the student to contact you at the next grading deadline, or to just say 'Hi' if he or she sees you around.

Staff Meeting 8

Staff Responsibities

When I first began teaching, I found out quite unexpectedly that I was really managing a business. I learned (the hard way) that a class consists of special interest groups that have to be convinced to work together smoothly. Unlike a typical vice-president, though, I have other things to do with my time besides manage. So at some point, I try to make my staff more aware of what they can do to help out.

I begin by giving my staff an idea of the size and complexity of our organization. I describe not only the class, but also the people I rely on (our front and back office staffs, the computer support groups), and the people who rely on me (the University's records office, and the like).

Next, I ask the staff to try to define the jobs of each of these groups. What are the students supposed to do? Readers? TA's? The instructor? I usually find that each group's responsibilities will be defined rather narrowly.

Finally, I lead a discussion of the expectations each group has of the others. This is the interesting area of discussion, because new areas of responsibility suddenly become visible. I suggest that each group has *explicit* responsibilities that it is fully aware of: 'What do I do for others?' However, I also point out the many *implicit* responsibilities that are expected without being clearly asked for: 'What do I expect others to do for me?' My conclusion is that problems arise when members of a group aren't aware of the implicit responsibilities their jobs entail.

The missed responsibilities are usually subtle. For instance, I expect students to come to class having done the assigned reading. The readers expect the TA's to back them up when a problem arises in the terminal room. The TA's expect me to take care of bureaucratic hassles with their paychecks. The office staff expects to get positive feedback when things go well. None of these are part of the official job description, but they all contribute to the smooth running of the organization as a whole.

Handout

I use the attached Staff Responsibility handout to help start and structure the discussion. A circular list of the groups on the blackboard helps in clarifying the various cross relationships.

Doug Cooper   Staff Responsibility   Introductory Pascal

1) How many different interest groups are there in a class?

- instructor
- students
- TA's
- readers
- clerical support staff
- technical support staff

Are there others? Does the University have any particular interests in a given class?

2) How does each see his or her job? What are each group's responsibilities?

- instructor:
  Teaches the course, makes up assignments, gives grades.
- students:
  Study, suffer.
- TA´s:
  Give sections, hold office hours, help grade exams.
- readers:
  Consult in the terminal room, grade homework.
- clerical support staff:
  Make sure that forms show up, that handouts are copied, and that paychecks arrive.
- technical support staff:
  Keep the computers running.

3) In doing their jobs, each interest group relies on the members of other groups.

- Who relies on you? Who doesn't?
- What do you do for each of the groups identified above?

4) To get your job done, you need the help and cooperation of other groups.

- Whom do you rely on most? Whom can you get along without?
- What do you expect each of the other groups to do for you?

5) Organizations sometimes develop problems when a group's responsibilities are viewed differently by its members, and by the members of other groups.

- Have you ever felt that you were expected to do something that wasn't your job?
- Have you ever felt that somebody in another group made your job easier by going out of his or her way? How?

Staff

Most programming courses have three staff categories: *readers*, typically undergraduates whose nominal duty is grading homework; *teaching assistants*, usually graduate students who conduct sections separate from the regular lecture, and may have some influence in determining a student's grade; and *instructors*, advanced grad students or faculty who have the dual responsibility of educating students and directing the staff.

To a lesser or greater extent, the entire staff shares the job of running a course. I divide the work along these general lines:

Lecturing involves presenting new material or methods in lectures, in sections given as adjuncts to the lecture, and in directed, hands-on computer labs.

Advising reinforces the material presented in lectures, and helps the student deal with details and problems that come up in the course of completing assignments and preparing for tests. Advising takes place in sections, in office hours, in the terminal room, and in commentary on completed assignments or exams.

Certification helps the student evaluate her command of the subject and labels her accomplishments for the benefit of the school or a future employer. It's accomplished through grading of homework, lab work, and exams, and through subjective evaluations of ability as evidenced in lecture, section, or lab performance.

Motivation keeps the student working at the highest possible level. A conscious, continuing effort to motivate students makes the difference between teaching and mere lecturing.

I generally assume that staffing takes place in an environment of insufficient funding and talent that requires novel methods of obtaining staff, and of dividing their duties. Let me make some suggestions for acquiring and training staff.

Give academic credit. My university grants one unit of credit for each three hours of work, with per term and overall credit limits on such units allowed. Students typically sign up for three units (nine hours plus a one-hour staff meeting per week) of pass/no pass credit. Unless there are exceptional circumstances, all pass.

Form a club. An alternative to an organized 'teaching experience' course is to set up an independent or group study course run along the same rules. Other inducements may be computer club membership, additional machine privileges, etc. I usually recruit directly from the first or second major-line course during the last week or two of the prior term.

Let me interject a few words on behalf of undergraduate volunteers. Students who volunteer to be staff members are enthusiastic and motivated. Although they may lack the knowledge needed to lead discussions, or the judgement required to make subjective grading decisions, they are tremendously effective as 'peer advisors' in the terminal room. They delight in showing other students how to deal with system or program problems, and add a genuine air of excitement to the terminal room. Making them go away is one of the biggest problems; student volunteers have seldom before experienced the gratification of actually being able to help other people with their problems.

Pre-train potential paid staff. At Berkeley, we've developed a well-understood farm system. Paid positions require previous experience in one of the volunteer positions, or work in one of the less desirable positions (say, as a grader for a self-paced course). Graduate students are often required to take a one-hour weekly 'TA training' course. A less time-consuming alternative is to require potential staff members to attend a number of staff meetings in the prior quarter.

Have the experienced teach the novices. This is particularly useful for dealing with a large, inexperienced staff. I distribute the job of training to senior members of the staff. The head TA keeps an eye on the other TA's; visiting their sections and giving advice. An experienced 'reader leader' helps the novices along. Having a relatively experienced staff member act as a daily straw boss (described below), ensures that the operation runs smoothly from day to day.

Document the course. Although class notes may be useful for defining week-to-week course content, they do little to prepare a novice instructor or head TA for the difficulties of course management. I generally have a senior staff member (head TA or reader leader) take notes at each weekly staff meeting, then prepare a short writeup. The topics covered in these meetings are the real nitty-gritty of course management. The notes are collected at the end of the term, and can be passed on to the incoming staff or instructor. I can't stress too heavily how important such notes can be to revolving-door faculty who, whatever their competence and desire, arrive with no experience of local computing or staffing conditions.

Staff Numbers and Organization

I typically have a staff pyramid that contains one instructor, a number of section or lab leaders (e.g. TA's), and a larger group of graders and front-line consultants (e.g. readers). With any luck, there are experienced members at each level.

At Berkeley, sections usually contain about twenty students. The number of sections each TA teaches varies in response to course funding—when we're poorly funded, TA's work harder. Each TA will usually run anywhere from two to five sections per week. I assign a 10-hour/week TA as follows:

> 2 hours attending my lectures
> 1 hour preparing for section
> 3 hours giving sections
> 1 hour staff meeting
> 3 hours consulting/grading

Readers are allotted according to a University formula that allows six to twelve minutes per student, per week. Although this may be suitable for 'blind' grading, it leaves far too slim a student/reader ratio for successful face-to-face grading and terminal room consulting (which is why I recruit volunteers so strenuously). I divide 10 reader hours simply:

> 1 hour staff meeting
> 9 hours terminal room consulting/grading

At Berkeley, a course of 150 students might consist of one instructor, two or three TA's (at 10 hours/week each), and 30−35 hours weekly divided among three or four paid readers. In addition, the paid staff may be matched, or outnumbered, by volunteers. Our upper limit on course size, incidentally, has approached 300 students per term.

Staff Management

A clear staff hierarchy helps in handling large classes. It is important to assign authority concommittant with responsibility, and to avoid the tendency to meddle across staff lines. My hierarchy works like this:

- Readers have primary authority for grading homework. Grading criteria come from me. Objections to particular grades may be discussed with the reader leader, but not with TA's. The head TA is the final arbiter. Readers are responsible for short-time tracking of weaker students.

- The reader leader has authority to ride herd on the paid and volunteer readers. He is responsible for maintaining and enforcing work schedules, and for maintaining a semblance of order among staff use or abuse of course equipment. He calls on the head TA (or rarely, me) to be his enforcer.

- TA's have primary authority for grading examinations, and responsibility for giving sections. I set criteria, and appeals on grades are taken first to the TA, then to the head TA. TA's are responsible for longer-term counseling of weaker students.

- The head TA has authority over the TA's, and is responsible for their schedule and performance. He can call on me when necessary.

- As instructor, I have responsibility for everything. However, I try to refrain from exercising authority whenever possible. Instead, I concentrate on explaining what I expect in weekly staff meetings. I also act as 'honest broker' between the staff and the class, explaining what each should expect of the other, and bringing up misunderstandings during class or staff meeting time.

I find that this kind of setup avoids friction inherent to large numbers of students and staff. Readers are in charge of the terminal room, and homework grading; they answer to the reader leader, and are not responsible to TA's. TA's, in turn, are in charge of sections and exam grading; they answer to the head TA, and don't worry about me looking over their shoulders.

Most importantly, I try to avoid undercutting the authority of staff members. I keep an eye on what the staff does, and will try to expedite handling of student complaints if there are any. However, I refuse, say, to argue with students about homework or exam grades. One cannot win such arguments, and over the long run they lead one to take an unfortunately dim view of students.

Staff meetings are held weekly. I often have separate meetings for readers and TA's; the TA's have heard most of this before, and we can cover the week's section assignments quickly over coffee. The reader meetings, in contrast, involve a considerable amount of staff training. I believe it is very important for the instructor to conduct these meetings personally, instead of assigning them to the head TA. Staff members are grateful for the attention, and work much harder.

The overall theme of staff meetings is encouragement. I open by passing along favorable student comments, then ask for comments or requests from students to be passed back to class. Discussion of the week's problems comes next: How did the assignment go? Are students having particular problems? Was the system impossibly overloaded? Did course software work? Are there suggestions from me or the staff? Next, we discuss some special topic, then, we go over the next week's assignment. This requires a brief description of the assignment and its possible solutions, some suggestions as to student problem areas and good hints to give, then finally an outline of criteria for high, medium, and low grades (discussed in greater detail elsewhere).

Hours and Straw Bosses

Hourly staff assignment can be a problem when more than a handful of people are involved. In my courses, staff are usually found in the terminal room. Since there is no 'blind' or home grading, readers have nowhere else to be. My observation is that (unless lecture is absolutely awful) TA office hours are largely wasted, so I ask that TA's spend a considerable amount of time doing on-site consulting in the terminal room, too. In practice, I try to keep the terminal room staffed for as any hours as possible (e.g. 12 hours daily), doubling or tripling staff during crucial times.

Simple single coverage, at 12 hours daily, requires 84 hours per week. A hypothetical course of 300 students, funded at the rates suggested above (about 40 TA hours and 70 reader hours weekly) will just cover it. A 150 student course, with lower machine usage, could get by with six hours (2–9 P.M.) daily. Naturally, this is just a baseline for terminal room staffing. Duplication is absolutely necessary during peak times, such as homework due periods. *Recruitment of volunteers* is the only way things can work out.

Given volunteer help equal to or greater than paid staff, adequate supervision can be a problem. My solution is simple—I appoint a paid staff member to be straw boss for each day. The straw boss is required to keep the terminal room running for the entire day. This won't require a constant presence, but does imply that the straw boss know each day's staff schedule, and keep an eye on the room, either by showing up or calling in occasionally. The straw boss makes sure that the newer staff members know what they're doing, and reassigns or covers for open hours. This saves the instructor quite a bit of hassle in setting or rearranging schedules. It also appeals to the paid staff, who end up with plenty of lattitude over their jobs.

Sections

A section is a supplementary class meeting, usually given by a staff member once weekly. It is intended to help the student with regular class problems or homework, or to expand on more specialized material or applications. Section is differentiated from class primarily by size; it is small enough (15 – 25 students) to allow informal discussion.

Sections In C.S.

The computer science course can use the section toward a number of ends, limited only by the talent of the staff, or the effort the instructor is willing to put into preparing sections:

- Organized review of lecture.
- Question and answer session.
- Introduction to system features, e.g. the editor.
- Discussion of pending or past homework.
- Meeting time for group projects.
- Quizes.
- Discussion of non-mainline topics, e.g. cryptography.
- Presentation of examples that are too large for regular lecture.
- Discussion of programming techniques or algorithms.
- Tours of computing facilities.
- Discussion of hardware.
- Talks by working programmers or more advanced students.

Sections may be mandatory or voluntary. I find that section is usually mandatory when the TA is responsible for helping develop the grade of individual students. Under such circumstances, the TA may call roll, collect or return assignments or exams, or give quizes.

Voluntary sections are less formal. In fact, students need not even be assigned particular section times; all sections are considered to be open. The main problem with this loose arrangement is that students may crowd certain convenient section times; my solution is to reassign a less popular TA to those times.

In either case the TA gets to know many students by name, and students are encouraged to develop more personal 'consulting relationships' with individual TA's. My experience is that open sections are no less successful than mandatory sections for establishing cordial relations.

Problem Solving and Lecture Review: A Model for Sections

In my course, I want sections to reinforce the two areas students have most difficulty with—the mechanics of Pascal, and the development of an approach to solving programming problems. Despite their small size, though, some characteristics of section make teaching difficult. In a lecture, the silent rows of students we face remain fairly uniform. In contrast, section discussion is free and open, and differences between students of varying abilities are accentuated. The TA, often more than the instructor, finds herself in the difficult position of serving several menus at once. Slower students need to be able to ask what can appear to be trivial questions, or perhaps to request a recap of a prior section's or lecture's content. Medium students may be primarily concerned with the current week's assignment, and the best students may only wish to discuss new problems or topics.

My conclusion has been that a single section type doesn't suffice to complement my lectures—some students are bored, others are snowed, and there never seems to be enough time to deal with both. My solution has been to offer two types of open sections.

Lecture review sections summarize lecture material, encourage questions, and discuss particular difficulties associated with the system or the current assignment. The latter part of review sections can be used to introduce new topics if desired. I give the TA a Xerox of problems from the current chapter, and checkmark simpler problems that should be mastered. The TA can refer to and solve the problems, or can use them as illustrative answers for questions.

Problem solving sections are intended to teach just that. Again, I mark perhaps half a dozen problems (taken, of course, from *Oh! Pascal!*). This is too many to solve in fifty minutes; instead, the TA 'sets up' the problem for solution, then moves on to another. I instruct the TA to remember that students are often confused when they read English language problem statements. Her job, then is to show straightforward methods of jumping into programs. She employs three methods:

1. First, she reads the problem and develops a quick overall decomposition into major program parts (user instructions, input, calculation, etc.).
2. Second, she develops some trial code, on scratch paper, that takes care of the hard part—perhaps some central calculation or I/O.
3. Finally, she presents a rough draft of the program's pseudocode—just detailed enough to clearly point the way to a solution.

Note that although this may not be a classic example of top-down program development, it does mirror the process an experienced programmer goes through in the first few minutes of dealing with a problem. First she gets a handle on what the problem entails; second, she reassures herself that whatever algorithm is required is within her capacity; then finally she begins the real stepwise refinement or pseudocode process.

Is the rapid attack of several problems a good way to teach problem solving? Yes and no. Obviously, fully-developed examples with well-planned problem decomposition and stepwise refinement are necessary. They are well-suited for class, they exemplify the programming techniques we are trying to teach, and they are useful in helping the instructor introduce new programming or coding techniques. However, such large, well-developed examples work best with smart students who are able to develop faith in their ability to apply the same technique to different programs.

Unfortunately, big model examples can be of only marginal help to students with little faith or self-confidence. To these students, a well-developed stepwise refinement can appear to be the programming equivalent of a well-developed mathematical proof. The instructor seems to make a series of inspired guesses, then the steel door of 'Wasn't that easy?' clangs shut.

Does setting up several problems (without solving them) teach problem-solving? I believe that, if a section can be devoted to a sequence of four to six rapid demonstrations, the answer is a resounding yes. Face it—the intro CS student is in the exact same position as the tyro math or physics student struggling with word problems. Although approaches to dealing with such problems have been formalized (e.g. Polya) the majority of students learn the old fashioned way—practice, practice, practice. If a student becomes confused during any particular example, all is not lost; another is coming up in a few minutes. The first few steps are the most confusing, and the student is taken through these steps again and again.

In summary, my approach to section is to have open, voluntary sections of two types. Lecture review sections deal with the more basic difficulties of homework, Pascal, and system mechanics. Problem solving sections focus on stating and setting up programming problems, but are not too concerned with detailed code. In either case, the instructor should help the TA set her agenda by providing sample topics or questions.

Homework

Homework in CS courses has changed over the years because of increases in course size, the shift to interactive equipment, changed expectations of student ability, and a variety of other reasons. All instructors agree that homework is an essential part of learning to program, but there is a wide variety of opinion on size and frequency of assignments, attitude toward group work, cheating, grading policies, due dates, etc.

The Basic Issue – Mastery or Certification?

To me, the essential question in a discussion of homework is whether it's a tool to help the student master the material, or is a test intended to help certify her overall ability.

The argument for homework as certification suggests that (in CS in particular) homework programs reflect the real-life requirements placed on a programmer far more accurately than an examination might. Homework is the student's opportunity to demonstrate her ability, and certifies the extent to which the she has learned the subject matter. This is the model used in, say, English classes, which typically do away with final exams, and base grades entirely on homework graded on a rising scale.

Using homework to certify students has several implications. First, homework must count for a significant portion (40% or more) of the final grade. Second, there should be a relatively normal distribution of homework 'results;' some will do well, and others poorly. Third, toward this end, students can be given comparatively little individual help on the assignment. Fourth and finally, individual work will predominate, and there will be prohibitions against student collaboration.

The argument against using homework for certification argues that examinations *can* adequately distinguish between students who are potentially better or poorer programmers. In consequence, homework can be used as a tool for achieving, rather than certifying, mastery of a particular subject area.

This view, too, has implications. First, homework will count for a third or less of the grade. Second, the grade distribution will be dramatically skewed toward very high homework scores; in effect, the great majority of students will completely master the assignment. Third, toward this end, staff may give students a great deal of help, even to the point of 'giving away' the hard part. Fourth, and finally, students will be encouraged to fraternize, and group efforts will be common.

I incline toward the second view and use homework as a tool, rather than as a test, for several reasons. Although I have to fulfil my duty as the school's official CS certifier, I have trouble letting this obligation obscure a more fundamental desire to teach *all* students, not equally, but to the best of each student's ability. As useful as homework may be for certification, it is even more valuable as a tool for teaching. If I can find another means of certification (and I believe that testing can suit this purpose), I prefer to give each student the opportunity to master each week's assignment, even if she must be led by the hand.

My approach, then, is to make homework required, but low-key. Overall, homework counts for about a fourth of a student's overall grade—just enough to ensure that the student will do it, and to supply necessary psychological satisfaction about the 'importance' of an assignment. However, homework grades are quite high, averaging 90%

of the maximal grade. Thus, completed homework has little influence on a student's final grade. I find, incidentally, that this concept (that homework grades simply change the class baseline) should be carefully explained to the class if you want to avoid end-of-term arguments about grades.

Face-to-Face Grading

Face-to-face grading, where the student and grader go over the assignment jointly, arises as a natural consequence of using homework to ensure mastery, rather than to certify performance. Now, in 'blind' grading, a student turns in homework by a certain deadline, then receives it back (along with red marks and a grade) a week or so later. This is murder on the staff (who dread the thought of sitting down to a huge stack of programs), and of limited benefit to the student, whose post-inspection is liable to be limited to her grade.

In contrast, the face-to-face method lets the grader become actively involved with the most gratifying part of teaching—making students understand. The student gets immediate feedback on her work, and (especially in large classes) is given what may be the only personal attention she gets. The grader gets to know students individually, and is able to suggest that particular students work together, or that one help another out. In addition, since face-to-face grading takes place in the terminal room, graders are available as consultants during slack periods.

All-in-all, face-to-face grading is such a win that it I can't conceive of going back to the old system. If you've never tried it, let me encourage you to take the plunge—it is probably the single most important improvement that can be made in course management.

There is, of course, another recognized approach to grading—computerized grading. I find that this method loses on several fronts. It encourages 'result-oriented' assignments, in which solution of a particular problem, rather than development of a general method, is the goal. Worse, automated methods for evaluation of subjective values (quality of identifiers or comments, use of procedures, etc.) are valid only by very specialized criteria, and are wide open to subterfuge in any case.

Grading

Whether homework is used to teach or certify, establishing consistency in grading is difficult since graders, almost by definition, are the least experienced staff members. As the number of criteria used to determine the grade increases, fairness becomes progressively harder to attain. I solve the problem by fiat, decreeing a conceptual three-point scale. An individual student's work may be very good indeed, or not really too good at all, or somewhere in the middle. My experience is that, using such a scale, consistent judgement is remarkably easy to obtain.

This does not mean that I don't establish a wide range of criteria for evaluating a program's goodness. The grading checklist supplied elsewhere shows that these can be quite detailed. However, such criteria are used as the basis of suggestions for students, rather than as strict determinants of point values. In practice, I find that a fairly cursory inspection gives the grader an opinion of whether the program is above, below, or at, the average. Then, instead of computing a program's grade by summing or subtracting points, the grader points out individual criteria that justify his overall reaction to the program.

Thus, the grader first looks the program over to get a general feel for its quality. Then, she reads it more carefully, runs it and asks the student questions, etc. Criteria are cited along the way: 'I have to take off a point for poor identifiers, but I'll add one for good commenting...' Miraculously, the total turns out to justify the reader's initial subjective evaluation.

Naturally, not all flaws are cited. Rather, the reader deducts points in areas that it is within the student's capacity to particularly concentrate on for next time. Similarly, positive comments are used to reward and encourage the student. I usually urge the reader to single out some feature for special congratulation or 'extra' points.

Actual implementations of the excellent, medium, bad system vary. The '+, ok, −' method is the easiest, but I think it makes grading too cursory a process. I prefer to grade on a 20-point system, with the following ground rules. First, nobody gets 20. For mysterious reasons this cuts down on student grade gripes, and also lessens the tendency for students to go to absurd lengths to get a perfect score. Second, I set the point value of excellent, medium, and poor weekly; perhaps at 19, 17, and 15 points. 16's and 18's are given for borderline cases, and there are no half points. This seems to make the grader's job easier. Third, 12 is the minumum grade, given to anyone who shows up with an incomplete program (and 0 for those who don't make it at all).

In advising my readers on how to interact with students during grading, I make the following suggestions. They must recognize that grading is a time of tension for students, often exacerbated by time they have wasted in waiting. Taking 15−30 seconds to say hello to the student, to find out her name, and to make some comment ('Sure is busy today') produces excellent results. The reader must also understand the student's tendency to personally identify with her program; grading homework is a far cry from egoless programming! Any method that minimizes this identification is encouraged—referring to 'this' program or bug, rather than 'your' program or bug, is a good first step.

I also constantly remind my staff that a program's appearance may have only a loose correlation with the amount of effort a student, particularly a weak student, has put into it. Each student must be accorded proper respect. Her program may be a piece of junk, but it's a piece of junk that plenty of hours have gone into. Forgetting this is not bad because it hurts the student's feelings, but because it undermines her motivation to continue to work hard, and reduces her likelihood of listening to anything the grader is liable to say. It creates a far less satisfying interchange for the reader.

Most staff interaction with students occurs in the context of homework consulting or grading. Instructions to staff are discussed in detail in the section that deals with weekly staff meetings. Handouts for staff meetings are supplied there as well.

Exams

Like much of the intro CS course, our exams differ from those given in other curricula. Basic issues that other faculty have long since made their peace with are still being actively debated in computer science. Just what does a given question test? Is the examination supposed to indicate knowledge or potential, demonstrated ability or future facility? Even the medium in which the exam is given is open to discussion.

But aside from philosophical questions, practical considerations make devising exams hard. What questions will we ask, and how can our staffs grade them consistently? How long should it take to evaluate an exam, and can hard questions be made easy to grade? Does each student have a fair shot going in, or does the exam unfairly discriminate against some sort of students?

In practice we can find a great variety of response to these issues. However, I think that there are two general families of solutions to the examination problem, which start from two basic assumptions—either the exam is solely intended to evaluate and certify the student, or it's used to help the student learn as well. I assume by the way, that the examination is intended to distinguish between students (particularly the successful ones), rather than being given as a pass/fail test.

Basic Exam Philosophies

I've usually found that when certification is the primary goal, the student's ability at the very end of the term is of chief concern, and a big final exam is the method of measurement. Since the final is seldom returned to the student (and her account is turned off immediately anyway) the exam itself is not intended to be a learning experience. A large final typically represents a high percentage (60% or more) of the student's grade.

When testing is consciously used as part of the teaching process instead, I generally see a sequence of exams, with one or two midterms preceding the final. A large proportion (50%–90%) of the student's grade may come from testing, but this fraction is distributed among several exams (say, 20%, 30%, and 40% for a 90% exam total).

Fair Testing

In either case we're concerned that tests be fair. However, factors other than obvious bias or inconsistency can make a test unfair. Just what does 'fair testing' imply?

- That the test can be graded objectively, not subjectively, by different staff members.
- That the test does not inadvertently measure qualities that may be considered incidental, are of minor importance, or which are better tested elsewhere; for instance, the student's ability to perform under exam conditions, to perform in limited time, or to recover quickly from rattling incidents (discovery and announcements of errors in the test itself).
- That the test is equally accessible to all students; in particular, that poor wording of questions does not challenge a non-native's ability to speak English.
- That students have the same expectations of the test's contents; in other words, that first-timers aren't left in the dark while other students who have taken a prior course (perhaps in high school) have some familiarity with test problem-types.

- That the test not measure arbitrary sorts of knowledge simply because they are easily evaluated; e.g. questions on minor syntax, or peculiar output formats.
- Finally, and most importantly, that the test fairly determine each student's ability as students or programmers—that the questions, no matter how neat a normal distribution they may provide, actually measure the talents we're looking for.

It is now somewhat easier to see the motivations of the big final *vs.* sequence of exams parties. An instructor who has faith in both her test, and her students' ability to take it, will seek the reduced overhead of a single large test. In contrast, a teacher with less faith in both her students' ability to demonstrate, and an exam's ability to measure, will incline toward a number of tests.

It is no surprise that, in response to the considerations listed above, a number of schools have gone to the degenerate case, throwing up their hands and saying 'We can't solve it!' In these schools the entire course is considered to be a 'mastery' program; the final exam or project is graded pass/no pass.

My Model

My experiences have led me to be an apostle of little faith. I give two midterms and a final, for 15%, 25%, and 35%, respectively. Thus, 75% of the grade comes from exams, with the remaining fourth accrued through homework. Let me stress that I believe that my final examination alone can accurately distinguish between greater, average, and poorer abilities *for a homogeneous group of students*. However, my students have always been awfully heterogeneous (which is the main reason I enjoy teaching). As a result, I simply can't justify evaluating them on a single performance. Here are some of the considerations that have led me to giving several tests:

- Students sometimes have bad days; esp. during exams. Sure, everybody's under the same pressure, but some react more severely than others, and I'm not trying to measure performance under pressure. I'll even grant that students (especially majors) will have to take tests under high pressure later. But that's exactly why I give my students (usually freshmen) the opportunity to learn to perform under pressure via a sequence of tests.
- Most students have absolutely no idea of what a CS examination is like. Some pick up rapidly (especially if they've taken any kind of computer course before), but others don't. I view the first test as being a practice exam of sorts, with the second serving a lesser, but similar role.
- Schools generally have fairly early deadlines for dropping classes, or for changing individual grading options from letter grade to pass/no pass. I think that we're obligated to give the student an early tentative evaluation, and with it the opportunity to make an informed choice about her future in the class.
- Just as I help teach the student to take tests, I have to train the staff to grade tests, and I prefer to have them practice on less crucial exams! More seriously, though, the difficulty of grading an exam is in direct proportion to its weight in the course. I find that grading is easier to do, and more consistent in outcome, when I've been able to develop a semi-experienced staff, and when no single problems stand out as large arbiters of the student's grade.

- Finally, my students have seen four tests by the time they take the final—two midterms, and two samples (usually the midterms of the previous term). Tests are different enough that I don't feel I'm just teaching them to test well. However, the necessity of preparing for midterms gives the students formal anchor points for organizing, then assessing, their knowledge and ability.

Interpreting Grade Distributions

Student abilities may vary greatly from those of the general public, or even between one course and another. However, in any one classroom we expect to find a normal distribution of talents; some students will be better, some will be worse, but most will fall in between. A normal grade distribution will look like this:

Its main characteristic is that the average grade (the *mean*) approximates the most frequently given grade (the *mode*). Moreover, this grade is the *median* as well; about half the grades are higher, while half are lower. Note that this particular grade need not lie at the 50% mark. A harder test might move the mean/mode/median grade 20 points to the left, while an easier test will cause a similar shift to the right. In either case, the curve maintains its characteristics.

As implied earlier, a normal distribution on a test result is pleasing to the instructor because it means that her test is 'fair.' The test might be a little too hard or too easy, but overall it confirms her everyday classroom experience that some students can answer all questions, most can answer many questions, and some can answer hardly any at all.

When the normal distribution begins to get warped toward either extreme we'll see distributions that are skewed like these:

These results are somewhat less satisfying because we find a larger than expected proportion of students doing very well or very badly. However, they're still acceptable because it's hard to design a perfect test. But when results are really skewed they become objectionable:

What can we infer from these test results? There's always the possibility that the students haven't obliged by displaying a normal range of talent. A much likelier possibility is that the test was poorly designed or evaluated. In the left-hand test, above, it is quite clear that the questions were too easy. As a result, the better students haven't been given the chance to demonstrate their talents; they fall into the mass of 'pretty good' students who have gotten near-perfect results.

The right-hand test fails in the other direction; too many students are lumped into the 'poor' category. One explanation is that questions were just too hard, and that even average students couldn't measure them. But a second cause can lead to the same left shift: grading high-value questions without granting partial credit. Suppose that a student attempts to complete the entire test. If she has to work quickly, and doesn't have time to check her results, she'll get a low grade. Changing her strategy by taking the time to check and double check her answers leads to the same effective result—she hasn't had time to complete the test.

Finally, grades from introductory courses often display the bimodal distribution shown below:

A curve like this implies that a class contains not one, but two, normal distributions of students, one stronger and one weaker. Although this may actually be the case in specialized circumstances (as when a course contain half CS major whizzes and half computer literacy hopefuls), for the vast majority of classes the 'inherent bimodal distribution' argument defies reason. In fact, a variety of reasons, including poor teaching, can lead to bimodal distributions. Some problems, and suggested cures, are:

- Problem: Insensitivity to the class's reactions, or a lack of feel for their level of understanding. Cure: Spend a few hours in the terminal room every week.
- Problem: Unrealistic expectations of student performance. Cure: Recognize that intro CS is a very widely taken course that's no longer limited to those with science backgrounds or strong hacker tendencies.
- Problem: Aiming the course at the best students, or feeling that it's the student's obligation to keep up. Cure: Try to restrict elitist attitudes to honors courses. Recognize the difference between lecturing and teaching.
- Problem: Splitting the test between easy and very hard questions. Cure: Try to present a range of questions, and prepare graders to give partial credit.
- Problem: Asking a small number of questions that require a particular insight for solution, making partial credit difficult to obtain. Cure: Try to make sure that test problems are susceptable to decomposition, and don't have a hard first step that effectively bars entry. Similarly, avoid high-value problems that are difficult unless a clever technique is used.
- Problem: Peculiar grading practices, particularly those that invite inconsistency. Cure: Avoid high-point 'all or nothing' questions, and monitor graders to make sure that they aren't tending toward

extremes.

- Problem: Asking too few questions. Cure: Ask questions that probe a range of student abilities. A particular problem with too few questions is that, if the instructor misjudges a problem (i.e. includes a 'bad' problem as we all do sometimes), the exam has little ability to absorb the error.
- Problem: Unequal student response to examination. Cure: Give out sample tests, or have a low-value warmup be part of the overall test sequence.

Facts *Every* Teenager Should Know About *Vi*

Copyright © 1985 by Doug Cooper

Vi is an interactive, screen-oriented text editor. *Vi*—visual, pronounced vee eye—was originally one of the modes of the *ex* editor (the other modes were *open*—a one-line form of *vi*, and *command*—for line-oriented commands). It is probably the most widely used of the Berkeley UNIX enhancements.

Text editors like *Vi* are used to create new files, and to inspect or modify existing files. *Vi* is not a word-processor, in the sense that it does not format text. Instead, *Vi* (like its predecessors *edit*, *ed*, and *ex*) provides powerful commands for interactively making small or large-scale changes in a file's contents. Other UNIX editors, like *sed* and *awk*, are better suited for batch-oriented editing.

A brief history of computer editing will make learning about *Vi* a little easier. As you might imagine, ideas of what text editing involves, and the tools used to make it happen, have always been closely tied to technology. Back in the days of punched cards, there were no text editors, because punching a card was the computer equivalent of chiseling in stone. A card containing an error was thrown away because there was no way it could be fixed.

Hard teletypes, which printed on paper, brought computer editing into the cuneiform age. The paper output is simply a description of text stored in the computer's memory. (In contrast, punched cards actually held the text of, say, a program, and needed to be read into the computer before each use.) Since a computer stores information in the form of magnetic or electronic impulses, it's as easy to alter stored information as it is to magnetize, or change the magnetic polarity of, a ten-penny nail.

Editors for hard teletypes required a user to type in a description of the change she wanted to make, and were sometimes called 'descriptive' editors. For instance, changing the word 'Annette' to 'Renee' required a command like '*substitute/Annette/Renee/*,' which described both the old and new forms of the text.

The invention of CRT's brought computer editors to the age of CorrecType. Video screens, unlike printing teletypes, allowed invisible erasing. Editors were devised that let a user modify the current line before committing it to the computer's memory. (We can see the same sort of technology in typewriters that let you work on a single line electronically before hitting an 'Output' key that actually types the line.) Nevertheless, early CRT editors were quite similar to teletype editors. They generally allowed only descriptive commands, and were oriented toward working on single lines of text.

A small improvement in the design of electronic terminals made a new form of editing possible—screen editing. The original CRT's were often called 'glass teletypes' because, like teletypes, they only went in one direction. As each succeeding line was printed, it pushed its predecessors toward the top of the screen and eventual oblivion. The cursor, which is a terminal's equivalent of a teletype's print head, was effectively fixed at the bottom line of the screen.

In the late 70's, though, improved CRT's with movable cursors became cheaply available. A cursor could be positioned anywhere on a terminal screen, and allowed full screen-oriented editing, rather than single-line editing. Screen editors preserve the descriptive, line-oriented commands developed in earlier systems. However, they also let a user move the cursor around a screenful of text as easily as she might move a pencil around a page. For instance, a word can be deleted by moving the cursor to the word, then giving a 'delete' command. There is no need to describe the word to the editor by spelling it out. The delete command just deletes all characters from the current position to the end of the word (i.e. to the next blank space).

Vi is one of the most widely used screen editors. It understands both descriptive and screen-oriented commands, and can be used on many kinds of terminals and teletypes. This tutorial covers everything you'll need to know for your first few months of editing.

Vi Tutorial

In learning to use *Vi*, it's important to bear in mind that editing commands are intended to be simple and easy to remember. Where do commands come from? Some are preserved from earlier generations of editing systems. These commands were kept in *Vi* so that older programmers wouldn't have to learn an entirely new system. Most *Vi* commands, though, are single letters that stand for what they do.

Although we'll only learn about 30 editing commands in this tutorial, *Vi* contains literally dozens of possibilities. When you try to remember *Vi's* abilities, and the names of its commands, it's helpful to know how its designer (a former Berkeley graduate student named Bill Joy) went about designing the system. First, he named all the obvious operations—*a* for *add*, *c* for *change*, *d* for *delete*, etc. Then, he looked at the remaining letters to see if they suggested commands—*G* became *go to some line*, *p* became *put text back*, *y* became *yank some text and save it*, etc. Finally, he looked at the remaining letters and let his imagination run wild—*f* led to *find some character*, *o* turned into *open a hole in the screen*, *}* became *go to the next paragraph*, etc.

Getting In and Out

The first thing to learn about an editor is how to enter it, and how to get out. The UNIX command:

%   **vi** *FileName*

invokes the editor on a file named *FileName*. Naturally, you'll give the name of an existing file you want to edit, or of a new file you want to create—after all, adding something to nothing is a form of editing.

If *Vi* is invoked on a file that doesn't exist yet, you'll get a blank screen, and a message to that effect:

%   **vi** *Annette*
-

-

-

"Annette" [New file]

The tilde (˜) indicates a non-existent line. You'll probably get a whole screenful of them.

If *Vi* is invoked on a file that does already exist, the file's first page will be printed, along with a message about the file's length:

```
%   vi Patti
```
Although I once had a crush on the model Patti Hansen, I felt
that her marriage to Keith Richards removed her from serious

       (*more of the file goes here*)

all, if she were so inconsiderate as to marry a Rolling
Stone, and the dumbest one at that, I could hardly be expected
"Patti" 147 lines, 6750 characters

In either case, you'll find the curser at the upper left hand corner of the
screen. *Vi* is ready to be given commands.

    Getting out of *Vi* and back to UNIX is easy, but it requires a
special kind of command—one of the commands left over from the days of
descriptive editing. Now, *Vi* commands are usually invisible, and don't
appear on the screen when you type them. The old commands, though,
print on the bottom line of the screen. Every descriptive command
begins with a colon (:), which causes the curser to jump to the screen's
last line. When the command is finished, the cursor goes back to where
it belongs.

    Each descriptive command ends with the ESCAPE key (often
marked *esc*), although a carriage return will work just as well. The
command for leaving *Vi* is *x*, for *exit*:

```
:x <esc>
%
```

Moving Aroung

Screen editors like *Vi* are most appreciated for the ease with which they
let us move around a file. The simplest motion commands allow
movement one space, or line, in any direction. They are:

    h   back one space
    l   forward one space
    j   down one line
    k   up one line

These particular letters were chosen because early versions of *Vi* were
developed on a terminal (the ADM3a) that had little arrows on these
keys. Many modern terminals have explicit arrow keys that will work
just as well as **h**, **j**, **k**, and **l**. Remember that, unlike the descriptive
entry and exit commands, movement commands don't print on the
screen.

    Now, because *Vi* is usually employed for typing in English, it's
reasonable to assume that *Vi* will understand the concept of words. The
word motion commands have pretty obvious names:

    w   forward one word
    b   back one word

How about bigger motions? Suppose that we want to move forward
three words, or ten or twenty? As I mentioned before, it's often a good
idea to put yourself in the designer's shoes when you try to understand
Vi. How would you build such commands into the system?

    The solution—which applies to all commands that might require a
number—is to let a number precede the actual command. Moving ahead

five words takes the command '5w', and moving down twenty-two lines would be '22j'.

The final movement command makes it easy to go to a particular line.

#G   go to line number #
G   go to the last line

The use of **G** to move to the last line is a convenience built into *Vi*. It's kind of necessary since you might not know exactly how many lines a file has.

Examples to try

10b	go back ten words
3j	go down three lines
25G	go to line twenty-five
G	go to the very last line of the file
15h	go fifteen spaces to the left
10000G	What happens?

Getting Rid of Things

The basic deletion command is **d**. By itself, **d** doesn't do anything. The delete command is generally used in conjunction with one of the motion commands, to get rid of a word, space, etc. If the delete command is doubled, an entire line is removed.

d   delete one or more of **h, j, k, l, w,** or **b**
dd   delete an entire line

For example, we'd delete a word with **dw**, a space with **dl**, and an entire line with **dd**. A special (and not wholly unexpected) case—**dG**—allows deletion of the remainder of the file, from the current line on.

In any form, the **d** command can also be given a 'how many?' number. This number can go in either of two places with the same effect—**d2w** and **2dw** each delete two words, and **d5d** and **5dd** both get rid of five lines.

What goes in the place of a deleted line? Well, some terminals will redraw the screen very quickly, so that subsequent lines just move up. Other terminals print the 'something was here but not any more' character '@', e.g.:

There was a line below here...
@
But I deleted it.

You may recall that '~' serves a similar purpose for nonexistent lines that have never existed.

Examples to try

d5b	delete the previous five words
dd	delete the current line
dw	delete one word
d10d	delete ten lines

Adding and Changing Text

Before we can really have fun editing, we must know how to add text to a file. Now, if you stop and think for a moment, you'll see that any 'add text' command needs two basic features. First, we have to indicate where we want the new text to go—after or before the cursor, on the previous or next line, in place of one or more spaces, words, lines, etc. Second, we need to be able to *stop* adding. There must be a command that tells *Vi* that we're through adding text.

The first problem is taken care of with a series of 'append' commands, most of which are reasonably named. Solving the second problem—telling the editor when we're through adding new stuff—takes a special key we've already encountered. *Vi* uses the ESCAPE key, which is usually marked *esc*.

All these commands are ended with the <*esc*> key

a	add text after the current cursor position
i	insert text before the cursor
o	open up the next line—add after the current line
O	open the previous line—add before the current line
c	change one or more of **h, j, k, l, w,** or **b** (**cw** changes a word, **c3w** changes 3)
cc	change the entire current line (**3cc** or **c3c** changes 3 lines)

In fact, the <*esc*> can be used to end or interrupt most commands. For instance, if you were typing **d5w** (to delete five words) but mistakenly began to type **d555**, hitting <*esc*> will kill the partially formed command.

Examples to try

a	start appending after the cursor
o	append to a new line after the current one
c5w	change the next five words
c3c	change the next three lines

Undoing Mistakes, Saving Changes

Perhaps the most clever feature built into *Vi* lets us undo the last command:

u	undo the most recent command

For instance, suppose we were to delete fifty lines of text (with the command **d50d**), then reconsider our hasty move. The **u** command puts them back, as long as we haven't done anything else in the meantime. What do you think would happen if we hit **u** once more? It would undo the undo, and take the fifty lines away again.

Saving changes is usually taken care of automatically when you leave the editor. The **:x**<*esc*> command preserves all the editing changes you've made, and takes you back to UNIX. Unfortunately, sometimes computer systems crash, or terminals become disconnected, or phone lines mysteriously hang up. If this happens, any changes made between the start of the *Vi* session and the unexpected interruption will be lost unless you periodically *write*, or preserve, the file you're working on:

:w<*esc*>	save changes without leaving *Vi*

It's a good idea to issue a :w<*esc*> command every five or ten minutes, or after typing in twenty or thirty lines, just in case something terrible happens. Don't forget that, if you're currently adding or changing text, you have to type the <*esc*> key to quit adding. If you don't the :w will appear as part of your file.

Marking Lines, Finding Patterns

As we've seen, *Vi* contains a number of commands from the old line-oriented editors. In using these commands, it's usually necessary to specify exactly the lines of text that will be affected. We can either give explicit line numbers, or use the line number synonyms or 'marks' described below.

There are two commonly used synonyms for line numbers:

.   the number of the current line
$ the number of the last line in the file

In addition, two commands are employed to mark lines. The numbers of these lines are saved internally by the editor—we can refer to them if we want, but we don't have to remember the exact line numbers.*

ma   mark the current line 'a'
mb   mark the current line 'b'

We refer to a marked line with a single quote followed by the line's name. In the absence of any other command, the reference means 'go to' that line—**'a** means 'go to the line marked a.' Try experimenting with this feature—try **c'a** or **d'a**. Be sure to mark a line first, though.

In editing jargon, a word is a *pattern*, or any sequence of characters. Editors are very good at finding patterns, and it's usually easier to look for a pattern than to try to remember a particular line number:

:/pattern <*esc*>

The pattern may contain spaces, and need not be a whole word. Don't forget about capitalization, though. The colon that begins a pattern search command is optional.

Examples to try

'a   go to the line marked 'a'
d'b   delete lines from here through the line marked 'b'
ma   mark this line 'a'
c'b   change everything from this line through the line marked 'b'
:/Patti <*esc*>   Find the pattern 'Patti'
:/tti Han <*esc*>   Find the pattern 'tti Han'

Making Multiple Substitutions

Now that we have a convenient method of marking lines, it's time to learn a series of commands for making big changes in a file. The first allows multiple substitutions. This might come in handy in a program or paper if you've periodically misspelled some word or identifier.

---

* If you're really clever, you'll see that I've really shown two examples of the **m** command. A line can be given any one-letter name.

Substitutions are made by giving patterns. A pattern is any sequence of characters; to make a substitution we need an old pattern (to be found) and a new one (to be put in its place). A substitution command also gives line boundaries between which the substitution should take place. Remember that . stands for the current line, and $ stands for a file's last line.

:1,$s/*old pattern*/*new pattern*/**g**<*esc*>   substitute in the entire file
:'a,'bs/*old pattern*/*new pattern*/**g**<*esc*>   substitute between lines 'a' and 'b'

When you give one of these commands—or any command that begins with a ':'—you'll notice that the cursor jumps to the last line of the screen. This is normal and expected. If you make a mistake, you can either backspace and correct it, or hit <*esc*> and go back up to the screen.

Notice the final **g** in the examples above. This is another holdover from the old days, and means that if *old pattern* occurs more than once on a line, every instance should be changed. If the **g** weren't given, then only the first instance of *old pattern* would be replaced by *new pattern*. This is really the sort of detail that gives computers a bad name, and its 'logic' isn't really worth remembering.

Examples to try

:1,.s/*old*/*new*/**g**<*esc*>
    substitute *new* for *old* from the first line to the current line
:1,$s/*Patti*//**g**<*esc*>
    substitute nothing (i.e. remove) for *Patti* in the entire file
:.,'as/*Patti*//**g**<*esc*>
    as above, between the current line and mark 'a'

Making Big Changes

The line-oriented commands are necessary for jobs involving whole lines of text. The marks we used above come in quite handy in conjunction with the *delete, move,* and *copy* commands.

:'a,'bd<*esc*>   delete all lines from mark 'a' through mark 'b'
:'a,'bm.<*esc*>   move all lines from mark 'a' through mark 'b'
:'a,'bco.<*esc*>   copy all lines from mark 'a' through mark 'b'

Deletion is simple—all lines between two given line numbers are removed. They can be put back immediately with the undo command **u**. Moving and copying are quite similar, except that a copy results in two copies of the original lines. One copy is in the lines' original location, and the other will be found following the line the cursor was on when the copy command was given.

Examples to try

:.,$d<*esc*>   delete all lines from the current line through the file's end
:1,.d<*esc*>   delete all lines from the first line through the current line
:1,.bm$<*esc*>   move all lines from the first through the current line to the file's end
:.,'bm1<*esc*>   move all lines from the current through the line marked 'b' to after line 1
:'a,.co1<*esc*>   copy all lines from mark 'a' through the current line after line 1

File Manipulation

The final few commands we'll learn deal with entire files. We've already seen two such commands—the :**x**<*esc* > command, which saves changes and leaves the editor, and the :**w**<*esc* > command, which saves changes without leaving *Vi*.

On occasion, we'll want to leave *Vi* without saving changes. Although the **u** command will nullify the most recent command, we're left with the problem of recovering from real disasters. The *quit* command, which must be followed by an exclamation point, gets you out of the editor without saving any changes.

> :**q**!<*esc* >   leave *Vi* without saving any changes

This is only effective to the most recent :**w**<*esc* >. In other words, if you give a :**w** command, and then immediately leave *Vi*, all changes will be saved.

Another command is used to merge two files together. In the process of editing one file, we may wish to 'read in' the contents of a second file:

> :**r** *file*   put a copy of *file* in the current file

The second, named *file* still exists independently, but now there's a copy of it in the file you're currently editing. This is very convenient in programming applications, since we'll frequently write and test subprograms in individual files, then incorporate them into a larger file that contains the main program.

One Last Command

Occasionally *Vi* will get confused about what is supposed to be on the screen. This is sometimes the fault of *Vi*, sometimes of the computer, and sometimes of the terminal itself. One of two commands puts the screen back into shape:

> <*ctrl*>*L*
> <*ctrl*>*R*   *redraw the screen*

Summary of *Vi* Commands

u	undo the last command
<ctrl>R **<ctrl>L**	redraw the screen (use if garbage appears on the screen)

h j k l	move left, down, up, or right
w	move ahead one word
b	move back one word
#G	go to line # (5**g** goes to line 5)
G	go to the last line

d	delete one or more of **h, j, k, l, w,** or **b** (**dw** deletes a word, **d3w** deletes 3)
dd	delete the entire line (5**dd** deletes five lines)

ma **mb**	mark the current line (used below)

All the remaining commands are ended by typing the <esc> key

a	add text after the current cursor position
i	insert text before the cursor
o	open up the next line—add after the current line
O	open up the previous line—add before the current line
c	change one or more of **h, j, k, l, w,** or **b** (**cw** changes a word, **c3w** changes 3)
cc	change the entire current line

:/*pattern*	find *pattern*, and go there
:1,$s/*old* /*new*/**g**	change each instance of *old* to *new*
:'a,'bs/*old* /*new*/**g**	as above, but only between marks *a* and *b*
:'a,'bd	delete all lines from mark *a* to mark *b*
:'a,'bm.	move all lines from mark *a* to mark *b* to after the current line (.)
:'a,'bco.	copy all lines from mark *a* to mark *b* to after the current line (.)

:r *file*	Put a copy of *file* into the current file

:x	leave **vi**, saving the changes you've made in the file
:w	save the changes without leaving—do this once in a while
:q!	leave vi without saving any changes—for real screwups only!

A Note on the Exams

This section contains typical first, second, and final exams from my course. It is intended only as a a starting point for first-time instructors; an outline that can be improved, or adapted to the demands of your own course. There are many alternative notions of what constitutes a proper exam; my only intention is to supply some idea of bulk, breadth, and question type in a series of exams that I've found to be successful for my course.

My course is the non-major introduction to programming in Pascal. Roughly 40% of my students take the course because it is required for admission to the undergraduate program in Business Administration (the hottest major at Berkeley). Of the remainder, perhaps half (about 30% overall) take the course pass/no pass. The average grade given in my class is B−; the course is perceived as cruel (because B− is thought of as being a relatively low grade) but fair (because few students are failed outright).

I generally have 200−300 students in my section (there are two lecture sections, plus a self-paced section, plus a major-path section overall). Grades on the exams invariably average between 60% and 65%, with a standard deviation of roughly 18−20. The curve always shows a bell-shaped distribution (whether I supervise grading or not!), and is certainly not bimodal.

The two midterms are given in 50-minute class sessions, while three hours are allowed for the final examination. The exams count for 15%, 25%, and 35% of the final grade, respectively. The midterms are admittedly long; top students will have time to answer all questions and check each answer as well, average students will not be able to check every answer, and poor students won't answer every question. Partial credit is given when appropriate.

A considerable amount of attention is paid to making questions easy to grade quickly and fairly. Key techniques are:

- a relatively small number of points are allowed per question;
- questions are quite specialized;
- when programs are called for, I supply a gross outline (usually a doubly-nested **while** or **for** loop) that ensures that the answer isn't too weird;
- I rely heavily on question types that involve the student's judgement, but not the grader's; e.g. 'what's the input?', or 'where's the bug?'
- when grading judgement will be involved, questions have clear guides for partial credit.

As a rule, I distribute the previous term's midterms before giving the current term's test. My experience is that, given the time pressure, relatively small changes in each question suffice to make the test appear entirely new. For the same reason, the tests are always open-book, open-note.

- 2 -

Doug Cooper   CS 8, Fall '84   Midterm #1   15% of total grade

Your Name Is _____

Your Login Name (Account Number) is _____

Books and notes may be used during the test.

You have 50 minutes to complete the exam.

Be sure that your name is on the top of each page. Make sure that you have every page.

This midterm counts for 15% of your final grade, so don't panic.

Partial credit will be given, so please SHOW YOUR WORK.

Cheating is not allowed. You will receive a grade of 0 on the entire exam, and be required to apologize to the rest of the class, if cheating is established.

If you have any questions, please ask. There are no 'trick' problems on this test.

Today's Artist: Tom Petty and the Heartbreakers

Today's Song: *Even the Losers Get Lucky Sometimes*

SCORE

Page 0 _____ (5)

Page 1 _____ (20)

Page 2 _____ (20)

Page 3 _____ (15)

Page 4 _____ (20)

Page 5 _____ (20)

Total _____ (100)

0. (5 points) _____

'What becomes of the broken-hearted,
Who had love that's now departed?'

Above, the most poignant musical question of all time (as asked by the immortal David Ruffin, former leader singer of the Temptin Temptations). Please answer.

---

1. (10 points, 1 each) _____

What is the output of each statement below? If any of the statements are not correctly written Pascal, write 'Error' instead of showing the output. Showing exact spacing between output values is not crucial for numerical values. Assume that we have made these assignments:

Letter := 'F';   Number := 15;   Sum := 6;

Writeln ("Hi gang!", Number, '!');

writeln (ord (Letter) – (ord (Letter) –1));

writeln (Number mod Sum);

writeln ('Sum' div 3);

writeln (Sum.3);

writeln (Letter, Letter, 'Letter');

writeln ('Oh no', 'not', 'Bobs'');

writeln ('Sum' Letter, Number);

writeln ('round (Number/Sum)');

writeln ((10 div (Sum mod 4));

---

2. (10 points) _____

Assume that some CS 8 midterm grades are kept in a file in the following format:

bc/79/B
fw/35/D
dd/94/A

On each line, the first entry (e.g. 'bc') is the student's account number. The second (e.g. '79') is her percent grade on a test. The third (e.g. 'B') is a one-character letter grade.

Write the code segment needed to read the sample file above, and print it in a more understandable form. Here's an example of what the first line of output should look like:

Student bc scored 79% and got grade B.

Your code segment should not include a program heading, variable declarations, etc.—just make up variables as you go along. It will be less than 10 lines long.

- 3 -

3. (10 points, 5 points each)

A. Here is a program segment:

```
for Outer := 1 to 5
do begin
    for Inner := 1 to Count
    do read (TheCharacter);
    writeln (TheCharacter);
    readln (TheCharacter)
    end;
```

Here is its input:

> It is a
> very, very good
> idea to have
> enough input for your
> programs.

What is the program's output? Print it alongside the code, above, and draw a box around it. If necessary, show a space as an underline ('_'). (HINT: The for loop 'for Count := 1 to 1 do action' will do action one time.)

B. Here is another program segment:

```
Start := 1;
Finish := 4;
for Counter := Start to Finish
do begin
    Start := 2;
    Finish := Start;
    writeln (Counter)
    end;
```

What is the program's output? Show it alongside the code, above. Put a box around your answer.

4. (10 points)

Rewrite this pair of assignment statements as a single assignment statement. Make your answer as simple as possible. Assume that all variables represent positive integer values.

```
Tennis := Golf/Tennis;
Tennis := (3 * Soccer) + Golf;
```

Do the same for this pair:

```
Tennis := 3 * (Soccer + Golf);
Tennis := Tennis - (Golf * 2)
```

- 4 -

5. (10 points, 2 points each)

Suppose that we define these variables:

```
var Ch, Let: char;
    Num, Val: integer;
```

and include this statement in a program:

```
readln (Ch, Num, Let, Val);
```

For each legal line of input shown below, print the values of Ch, Let, Num, and Val. Not all of the input lines are legal. If an input line is illegal, show the value that will cause a crash. Be sure to read your answers carefully.

All spaces in input are shown with an underline for each space.

7_Z_19	Ch___ Num___	Let___ Val___	Illegal Value___
14.339R	Ch___ Num___	Let___ Val___	Illegal Value___
6-4_4P	Ch___ Num___	Let___ Val___	Illegal Value___
-9T_9.7	Ch___ Num___	Let___ Val___	Illegal Value___
66_66_66	Ch___ Num___	Let___ Val___	Illegal Value___

6. (5 points)

This program contains two semantic bugs. Find them and either fix or describe each one.

```
program EvenCount (input,output);
{Find the number of even digits in a sequence of input characters.}
var Digit, Counter, EvenNumber, Limit : integer;
begin
    writeln ('How many numbers should I look at?');
    readln (Limit);
    writeln ('Enter a digit');
    readln (Digit);
    for Counter := 1 to Limit
    do begin
        EvenNumber := 0;
        case Digit of
            0, 2, 4, 6, 8 : EvenNumber := EvenNumber + 1;
            1, 3, 5, 7, 9 : ;
        end; {Digit case}
        writeln ('Enter a digit');
        readln (Digit);
    end; {Counter for loop}
    writeln ('The number of even numbers was ', EvenNumber)
end.
```

7. (10 points) ———

The constant *maxint* is predefined in every Pascal implementation. It represents the largest legal integer value that a Pascal program must deal with correctly for the purpose of integer arithmetic. In other words, every integer expression whose value is *maxint* or less must be evauated correctly. However, this doesn't necessarily mean that expressions with a value greater than *maxint* will be wrong, or cause an error.

Personally, though, I have always wondered about *maxint*. What is its value, exactly? What is the number that comes after *maxint*? Can a variable be assigned the number after *maxint*? Write a very short test program that will give us the information I need in order to answer these questions.

8. (10 points) ———

What was the **input** of program Test, below? Assume that its **output**, shown on one line, is:

FCEHF

Draw a box around your answer.

```
program Test (input, output);
var C, CC, CCC: char;
begin
   C := 'E';
   for CC := 'A' to C
   do begin
      read (CCC);
      C := chr ( ord(CC) + ( (ord (CCC) − ord ('A')) + 1) );
      writeln (C)
   end;
end.
```

9. (10 points) ———

The program shown below requires input values of different Pascal types. Read the program carefully, then list, in order, the types of the input values needed. Be sure to draw a box around your answer.

You should use one-letter initials instead of the full type name. So, if the program needed an *integer* input value, followed by two *char* values, and then a *real* value, your answer would be:

I C C R

```
program TypeTime (input, output);
var   A: integer;
      B: char;
      C: real;
procedure Reader;
var   B: real;
      C: char;
begin
   read (A,C)
end;
procedure InPutter;
var   C,B: integer;
begin
   Reader;
   readln (C)
end;
begin
   readln (A,C);
   Reader;
   InPutter;
   read (A,B,C)
end.
```

10. (10 points) ———

What does the following program print? Draw a box around your answer.

```
program Confuser (input, output);
var i,j: integer;
begin
   for i := 1 to 4
   do begin
      case i of
      3: for j := 1 to 3 do writeln ('easy');
      1: begin
            write (i);
            writeln ('hi, kids!')
         end;
      2: ;
      4: begin
            writeln ('credit');
            for j := 1 to i
            do write ('for you.');
            writeln;
         end;
      end
   end
end.
```

Doug Cooper   CS 8, Fall '84   Midterm #2   25% of total grade

Your Name Is _____

Your UNIX Account Name Is _____

Books and notes may be used during the test.

You have 50 minutes to complete the exam.

Be sure that your name is on the top of each page.

This midterm counts for 25% of your final grade, so only panic slightly.

Partial credit will be given for wrong answers, so please SHOW YOUR WORK.

Cheating is not allowed. You will receive a grade of 0 on the entire exam, and be required to apologize to the class, if cheating is established.

If you have any questions, please ask. There are no 'trick' problems on this test.

This exam has 6 questions. Make sure your copy contains all of them.

ADVICE: Read through the test before starting work. Answer the questions you can deal with easily first. There are 100 points possible, so allow about 5 minutes for each 10 points. Pace yourself. If you can't deal with a question at all, leave it for last.

SCORE

Page 0   (1) _____

Page 1   (21) _____

Page 2   (21) _____

Page 3   (17) _____

Page 4   (20) _____

Page 5   (10) _____

Page 6   (10) _____

Total   (100) _____

0. (1 point) _____

'I know what you're thinking ...'Did he fire six shots, or only five?' Well, I guess the question you've gotta ask yourself is ....'

Above, Clint Eastwood's most famous quote (from *Dirty Harry*). What *is* the question you've gotta ask yourself at times like this?

1. (21 points, 7 points each) _____

Each of the following program segments contains a bug or potential bug. What is it? Assume that all problems have to do with semantics–there will be no type clashes or syntax errors.

HINT: Make up some sample data, and mentally execute each program segment. Each bug can be described in a single sentence.

A) Count and average the number of values in a sequence. A positive number follows the last legal value.

```
Sum := 0;
Count := 0;
NextValue := 0;
while NextValue <= 0
  do begin
       Sum := Sum + NextValue;
       read (NextValue);
       Count := Count + 1
     end;
if (Count <> 0)
  then writeln ('The average is', Sum/Count);
```

B) Read and count spaces until a non-space is encountered.

```
Count := 0;
read (ch);
if (ch = ' ') then
  repeat
    read (ch);
    Count := Count + 1
  until (ch = ' ')
```

C) Read pairs of values, and print them in reverse. Any negative number ends the sequence.

```
read (N1, N2);
while (N1 >= 0) and (N2 >= 0)
  do begin
       read (N1, N2);
       writeln (N2, N1)
     end;
```

2. (28 points, 7 points each) _____

The four program segments below all need to be rewritten. For full credit, rewrite each segment in Pascal. For partial credit, write the solution in pseudo-code.

A) Rewrite this program segment using a single **repeat** statement.

```
read (First, Last);
while (First = Start) and (Finish <> Last)
  do read (First, Last)
```

B) Rewrite this program segment as two **if** statements.

```
if (Value < -5) or (Value > 5)
  then Value := Value * 2
```

- 3 -

C) Rewrite this program segment so that it uses a **while** statement, and does not use a **repeat** statement.

```
Count := -1;
repeat
  read (Number);
  Count := Count + 1
until Number < 0;
```

D) Rewrite this program segment as a single **for** statement. It should control a single *writeln* statement—no assignments or other statements will be necessary.

```
i := 25;
repeat
  i := (i div 5) - 1;
  i := i * 5;
  writeln (i)
until i <= 0;
```

3. (10 points) _____

What is the output of program Squares? Draw a box around your answer.

HINT: Make a table to keep track of the current value—and name—of each variable.

```
program Squares (input, output);

type L7 = (Lucy, Ricky, LawrenceWelk);

var a,b: integer;
    c: L7;

procedure Scramble (var a:L7; b: integer; var d: integer);
  var c: integer;
  begin
    c := d;
    a := succ(a);
    b := d+2;
    d := (c+b) -2;
    writeln (b, c, d)
  end;

begin {Squares}
  a := 3;
  b := 4;
  c := Lucy;
  Scramble (c, b, a);
  if c = Lucy
    then writeln (a, b)
    else writeln (b, a)
end.
```

- 4 -

4. (20 points) _____

Note: For these problems, deciding **what kind** of subprogram to use, as well as **what kind of** parameters to use, is part of the problem.

1) Write a subprogram *Power* that takes a number, and a power to raise it to, then returns the number raised to that power. All values concerned are *integers*.

2) Write a subprogram that changes the value stored in a *char* variable to the letter 'X' if the letter the variable currently represents is a capital letter.

For the following problem we have supplied a program outline. The solution to the problem requires you to add one or more statements to the program outline.

5. (10 points) **Modify** program *ProcessText* , below, so that it reads and echos text while obeying the following rules:

- Preserve the input line structure of text. However,
- Always print a carriage return before you print the character '#' (pound sign).
- Print a question mark (?) at the beginning of every INPUT line.
- Print a plus sign (+) at the end of every line.

```
        program ProcessText (input, output);


    begin


        while not eof
          do begin


            while not eoln
              do begin




          end; {eoln loop}




      end; {eof loop}



    end. {program}
```

6. (10 points) What is the *output* of program Mystery?

Sample input:

```
!This is a test%
!of the program%
$Mystery%
!and it%
$should work.%
```

```
program Mystery(input,output);

var ch : char;

begin
  while not eof
    do begin
      read(ch);
      if (ch <> '!')
        then begin
          if (ch <> '$') then writeln;
          write(ch);
        end
      else writeln;
      while not eoln
        do begin
          read(ch);
          if (not ((ch = '%') and eoln)) then write (ch);
        end; {eoln}
      readln
    end {eof}
end.
```

Doug Cooper   CS 8, Fall 1984   Final Exam   35% of total grade

Your Name Is _____

Your UNIX Account Name Is _____

Books and notes may be used during the test.

You have 3 hours to complete this exam.

Be sure that your name is on the top of each page, including extra pages.

This final exam counts for 35% of your final grade, so please panic if necessary. Try to keep it relatively quiet.

Cheating is not allowed. You will receive a grade of 0 on the entire exam (and probably flunk the course) if cheating is established.

This exam has 15 pages. Make sure your copy contains all of them, or you will be in big trouble.

ADVICE: Read through the test before starting work. Answer questions you can deal with easily first. All writing--program additions, etc.--should be very brief. Pace yourself. Good luck!

SCORE

Problem 0	(5) _____
Problem 1	(18) _____
Problem 2	(7) _____
Problem 3	(7) _____
Problem 4	(7) _____
Problem 5	(7) _____
Problem 6	(7) _____
Problem 7	(7) _____
Problem 8	(6) _____
Problem 9	(6) _____
Problem 10	(6) _____
Problem 11	(6) _____
Problem 12	(6) _____
Problem 13	(5) _____
Total	(100) _____

0. (5 points) _____

Suppose that this were a lottery ticket instead of a final exam. Grand prize is **$1,000!!** What will you do with the money if you win?

1. (18 points, 3 points each) _____

Each of the following program segments contains a bug or potential bug. What is it? All problems have to do with semantics--there will be no type clashes or syntax errors. Each bug can be described in a single sentence.

HINT: Make up some sample input data, and mentally execute each program segment.

For the first three segments, assume these type definitions and variable declarations:

```
type Holding = array ['A'..'R'] of integer;
     Storage = array [1..20] of char;

var Saved: Holding;
    Held: Storage;
    Current: char;
    i: integer;
```

A) Initialize an array to all fours.

```
for Current := 'A' to 'Z'
   do Saved[Current] := 4
```

B) Reverse the values stored in an array.

```
for i := 1 to 20
   do Held[(20-i) + 1] := Held[i]
```

C) Find the position the value -50 is stored in.

```
Current := 'R';
while (Current > 'A') and (Saved[Current] <> -50)
   do Current := pred(Current);
   writeln ('The -50 is in position', Current);
```

- 3 -

- 4 -

For each of the next six problems we have supplied a program outline. The solution to each problem requires you to add one or more statements to the program outline. You may have to declare additional variables as well. In some cases, you may want to add to a statement by making its execution depend on a condition being met.

2. (7 points) Modify program SomeLines to print every character on every line that does *not* begin with a question mark. Beware of possible empty lines in input.

```
program SomeLines (input, output);
var Ch: char;


begin


    while not eof
    do begin


        while not eoln
        do begin




        end; {eoln loop}


        readln;


        writeln


    end; {eof loop}


end. {program}
```

D)   Count the number of letters in a sequence. The last legal letter is followed by an 'A'.

```
i := 0;
repeat
    i := i + 1;
    read (Current)
until Current = 'A';
```

E)   Count the number of times the letter 'Z' appears in a sequence. The letter 'X' follows the last legal letter in the sequence.

```
i := 0;
read (Current);
if Current <> 'X'
then begin
    if Current = 'Z'
        then i := i+1
end;
read (Current);
```

F)   Count and average the number of values in a sequence. A number greater than zero follows the last legal value.

```
Count := 0;
Sum := 0;
read (NextValue);
while NextValue > 0
do begin
    Sum := Sum + NextValue;
    read (NextValue);
    Count := Count + 1
end;
writeln ('The average is', Sum/Count);
```

- 5 -

3. (7 points) Modify program OtherLines so that it reads but does **not** print lines of input text, obeying the following condition: If any line contains the character 'T' five times or more **do** print the characters on the very next line (but not this line).

```
program OtherLines (input, output);
   var Ch: char;

begin

   while not eof
   do begin

      while not eoln
      do begin

         read (Ch);

         write (Ch);

      end; {eoln loop}

      readln;

      writeln

   end; {eof loop}

end. {program}
```

- 6 -

4. (7 points) Assume that you are given many lines of text input. In addition to various words, some lines contain dollar amounts. Each dollar amount is always preceded by a dollar sign. A typical line might be:

   A+ $20.00(bargain). $1.00 rebate for early signups!

Modify program CashForCredit so that it prints the sum of values on, and average dollar value on, **only** the line that contains the **largest** sum of dollar amounts.

```
program CashForCredit (input, output);

begin

   while not eof
   do begin

      while not eoln
      do begin

      end; {eoln loop}

      readln;

      writeln

   end; {eof loop}

end. {program}
```

5. (7 points) Modify program **SmallestInEachColumn** so that it prints the smallest value in each column of the array. (HINT: Think about the array column-by-column, instead of row-by-row). For example, if an array (our example is smaller than the array in program SmallestInEachColumn) contains these values:

```
4    4    1    7
3    8    4    5
0    7    9    8
```

Your output should look roughly like this:

The smallest number in each column is:
```
0
4
1
5
```

```pascal
program SmallestInEachColumn (input,output);
const MaxRow = 15;
      MaxColumn = 23;
type Structure = array [1..MaxRow, 1..MaxColumn] of integer;
var Data: Structure;
    i, j: integer;

begin
{ Assume that the array has been initialized with meaningful data }

      for i := 1 to
         do begin

            for j := 1 to
               do begin

               end; {j loop}

            writeln

         end; {i loop}

end.
```

6. (7 points) Modify program **Farthest** so that it gets a number from the program user, then finds the number stored in the array variable Data that is farthest from this number, as well as its position in the array.

```pascal
program Farthest (input,output);
const MaxRow = 15;
      MaxColumn = 23;
type Structure = array [1..MaxRow, 1..MaxColumn] of integer;
var Data: Structure;
    i, j: integer;

begin
{ Assume that the array has been initialized with meaningful data }

      for i := 1 to
         do begin

            for j := 1 to
               do begin

               end;  {j loop}

         end  {i loop}

end.
```

- 9 -

7. (7 points) Modify program Table so that it prints the value stored in every other element of the Data array according to the following rule:

Print every other value, starting with the first, on even-numbered rows.
Print every other value, starting with the second, on odd-numbered rows.

```
program Table (input,output);
const MaxRow = 16;
      MaxColumn = 22;
type Structure = array [1..MaxRow, 1..MaxColumn] of char;
var Data: Structure;
    i, j: integer;

begin
{ Assume that the array has been initialized with meaningful data }

for i := 1 to
   do begin

for j := 1 to
   do begin

write (Data[i, j]);

end; {j loop}

writeln;

end; {i loop}

end.
```

- 10 -

For each of the next three problems, we have supplied a program. Your job is to determine what the program's *output* is, given the *input* we've shown. Be sure to draw a box around your answer.

8. (6 points) What is the output of program Change? Use underlines to show blank spaces. Assume that the input to Change is:

Love don't come easy

```
program Change (input, output);

const   BLANK = ' ';  {one blank space}
        LIMIT = 20;

type    String = array [1..LIMIT] of char;

var     Message: String;

procedure ReadString (var Mesg: String);
  {This procedure reads in one string's worth of characters.
   The var parameter Mesg is first initialized to all blanks.}

begin
  {Body of ReadString}
end;

function Length (Mesg: String): integer;
  {This function represents the length of its argument,
   minus any trailing (i.e. extra) blanks.}

begin
  {Body of Length}
end;

procedure Convert (var Mesg: String);
var     Temp: String;
        i, j: integer;

begin
    Temp :=                          {Initialize Temp to all blanks.}
    j := 1;
    for i := 1 to Length(Mesg)
    do if Mesg [i] <> BLANK
       then begin
            Temp [j] := Mesg [i];
            j := j+1
            end; {if statement}
    Mesg := Temp
end;

begin {main program}
    ReadString (Message);
    Convert (Message);
    writeln (Message)
end.
```

- 11 -

9. (6 points) What is the output of program Mystery? Spaces are underlined in the sample input. The sample input is:

No._it's_a_game_of_give_and_take.

```
program Mystery (input, output);
type w = array [1..2] of integer;
var ch: char;
    x: w;
    y: integer;
begin
  x[1] := maxint;
  x[2] := maxint;
  while not eoln
    do begin
       y := 0;
       read (ch);
       while not eoln and (ch = ' ')
         do read (ch);
       while not eoln and (ch <> ' ')
         do begin
            read (ch);
            y := y + 1
         end;
       if x[1] < x[2] then x[2] := x[1]
       if y < x[1] then x[1] := y
    end;
    writeln (x[2])
end.
```

10. (6 points) What is the output of program WhoKnows, below. Assume that these values are input to initialize the array:

```
31  12  42  34
11  22  12  13
24  14  11  42
32  24  43  44
```

```
program WhoKnows (input, output);
type BoardType = array [1..4, 1..4] of integer;
var Board: BoardType;
    i, j, newi, newj: integer;
    Treasure, Done: boolean;
begin
  for i := 1 to 4
    do for j := 1 to 4 do
       read (Board [i, j]);
  newi := 1;
  newj := 1;
  repeat
    i := newi;
    j := newj;
    Treasure := Board [i, j] = (10*i + j);
    Done := Board [i, j] = 0;
    newi := Board [i, j] div 10;
    newj := Board [i, j] mod 10;
    Board [i, j] := 0
  until Done or Treasure;
  if Treasure
    then writeln ('Treasure Found', i, j)
    else writeln ('No treasure')
end.
```

- 12 -

For each of the next two problems, we have supplied a program. Your job is to determine what the program's *input was*, given the output we've shown. Be sure to draw a box around your answer.

11. (6 points) What was the input of program Modify, below? There was at least one zero. Assume there is one space between each input and output number. The *output* of Modify is:

```
5   2   -3   9   -2   7   3   -1
```

```
program Modify (input, output);

var    a: char;
       b: integer;

begin
  while not eof
    do begin
       read (a);
       if a = '0'
         then begin
              b := 0;
              repeat
                read (a);
                b := b + 1
              until a <> '0';
              write (-b);
         end; {if}
       write (a)
  end; {while}
  writeln
end.
```

12. (6 points) What was the *input* of program Supremes, below? THERE ARE NO CAPITAL LETTERS IN THE INPUT. Assume that the program's output is as shown. Blanks are underlined, and should be underlined in your answer too. Output is:

you_can't_hurry_LOVE_NO_you've_just_got_to_wait.

```
program Supremes (input, output);

var ch: char;

begin
  repeat
    read (ch);
    if ch = '!'
      then begin
           read (ch);
           while ch <> '!'
             do begin
                read (ch);
                if ch in ['a'..'z']
                  then write (chr((ord(ch)-ord('a')) + ord('A')))
                  else write (ch);
                read(ch)
             end {while loop}
           end {if part}
      else write (ch)
  until eoln;
  writeln
```

- 13 -

13. (5 points) What is the output of program SamTheSham? Draw a box around your answer.

```
program SamTheSham (input, output);

type L7 = (Huey, Dewey, Louie);

var  a,b: integer;
     c: L7;

procedure WoolyBully (var a:L7; b: integer; var d: integer);
     var c: integer;
     begin
          c := d;
          a := succ(a);
          b := d + 2;
          d := (c + b) − 2;
          writeln (b, c, d)
     end;

begin  {SamTheSham}
     a := 3;
     b := 4;
     c := Huey;
     WoolyBully (c, b, a);
     if c < > Huey
          then writeln (a, b)
          else writeln (b, a)
end.
```

A Note on the Homework

This section contains a typical series of homework assignments from my course. Like the sample exams, this collection should be seen as an example of a method that works for me, but will certainly not meet the needs of all courses.

My class is a 3-unit non-major introduction to programming; it meets two hours weekly. Nominally, the University expects two to three hours of outside work for each credit unit. In my class, like most programming classes, students get full value for their tuition dollar.

In the early part of the term I require weekly assignments, while later, larger assignments have weekly milestones. Overall, homework counts for 25% of the student's course grade. In general, though, most students will get very high homework grades.

week	grade	comments
1	P/NP	using UNIX
2	P/NP	text editor, simple programs
3	P/NP	advanced editing, first procedures
4	P/NP	**case** and **for**. 'Advisory' grading.
5	no homework — first midterm	
6	5%	*boolean* statements, parameters
7–9	8%	first project — stream text formatter
10	P/NP	practice with arrays — second midterm
11–14	12%	second project — interactive text editor
15	no homework — final exam	

Although it pains me to admit that their Pascal will probably go the way of their high-school French, I think my students are much more likely to end up specifying software or managing programmers than writing programs. The overall goal of my assignments, then, is to give students experience in planning, working on, and testing fairly large programs. The early assignments set the stage: we concentrate on writing many small programs, and on comfortable transitions between programs and procedures, and vice versa. The first project introduces stub programming and program testing, while the final assignment is a large group project.

Grading the early assignments Pass/No Pass is a clever ploy to reduce student complaints about the relatively low weight (given the amount of time it takes) assigned to homework grades. In the early part of the term I take advantage of my students' enthusiasm; they are happy to do homework whether or not their grades require it. Later on, though, they need a carrot (or stick, depending on how you look at it). The projects are time-consuming, but from the student point of view, they are appropriately important in grade terms.

The group project requires special handling. I generally establish three-person groups on the basis of total midterm grades—one each from from the high, medium, and low groups. Although I don't label the group members as such, I don't beat around the bush either. I make it clear that I expect the better students to help their weaker brethren with Pascal, and the weaker students to help the better programmers with group work. 'Stand back and watch me do it' isn't allowed; each group member is expected to be able to explain the entire project at grading time.

To ensure fairness, and to avoid embarrassment to students without friends in the class, I neither require nor permit voluntary groups. One person usually flakes out in each group, so they are essentially two-person teams. Overall, the projects run over 1,000 lines of code.

I strongly recommend group projects, for a variety of reasons. There is the obvious attraction of having students experience first-hand the problems of group design, and of dealing with other people's code. Group projects reduce load on computing resources, as well as on terminal room consultants. Of particular importance to me is the fact that projects let weaker students gain experience working on programs far more difficult than their individual talents would allow.

A final word on cheating: I assign homework to give the student an organized approach to mastering the subject matter, rather than as a test of the student's facility in mastering it. Toward this end, I usually encourage collaboration between students on homework, which renders cheating a non-issue. I have two basic reasons for this approach.

1. Better students work together anyway. In my experience, mid-level students suffer most from prohibitions on collaboration. Better students have the wit to work together in undetectable ways.

2. Pursuing cheaters warps the relationship I want to have with my class. I want my class to be a meeting ground for explanation and understanding; not a continuing test of moral rectitude. I have seen instructors become obsessed with checking up on their students, and I have no desire to become a Captain Queeg.

As discussed elsewhere, I rely on face-to-face grading to ensure that the student has actually learned the assigned material. In any case, most of the grade is derived from exams, where cheating *is* effectively prohibited.

Doug Cooper   CS 8   First Week Assignment

Purpose

The purpose of this assignment is to give you practice in using elementary UNIX programs. Although most of the UNIX tools we'll use are easy to master, they can be confusing if you've never tried them before. With a little practice, you'll have UNIX down pat before you start writing programs.

The commands are all explained on the attached handout. Read through it before you start. It's hard to break the system, so don't worry about making mistakes!

The staff is under absolute strict instructions not to answer questions unless you know the name of the person sitting next to you, and are able to show at least 12 teeth when you smile. They will be counting.

Trying Commands

Try out some UNIX commands. Misspell one and see what happens. Use the character erase and line-kill characters.

1.   Find out today's date with the **date** command. Find out what commands you've given already with the **h** command.

2.   Where is the terminal room? What does the red button do? When is the wrong time to hit it?

Manipulating Files

You'll find that we've already put a number of files in your account.

3.   Print the names of the files in your account with the **ls** command.

4.   Print file fran on your screen with the **more** command.

5.   Make a copy of file fran named Temporary with the **cp** command. Remove file fran with the **rm** command.

6.   Rename file Temporary fran (i.e. move Temporary to fran) with **mv**.

7.   Send file fran to the Davis printer in 300 Davis. Send another copy of the file to the counter lineprinter in the basement of Evans. If you send it to the Evans counter printer, what box does your output go to?

Running Programs

A Pascal program is in file TestRun.

8.   Try to compile file TestRun with the **pi** command. You'll find that you have to change TestRun's name (to TestRun.p) in order to run it. What error message do you get otherwise?

9.   Run the compiled program a few times with the **px** command. Give it input names with different lengths.

Communicating With The Staff

'Adorable construction worker (married to dull MBA) seeks fun, literate, intellectual for periodic escape from humdrum domestic routine. Advanced degrees preferred, but will accept famous authors of all sorts. No tennis players, genetic Californians, or mayo-on-white-bread eaters, please. Write NYR Box 7235.'

10. Above: An advertisement from the Personals column of the New York Review of Books. Use the **mail** program to send me an ad you would place in the class newsletter if there were one. Be sure to wait for the mail program to ask for the subject of your letter. Your ad should say something about yourself; do *not* send me a copy of the ad given above. Don't forget to sign your letter to me!

11. Practice making suggestions. Send in a suggestion, or just an anonymous comment, using the **suggest** command. You can sign if you want to.

12. Change your password with the **passwd** command.

Doug Cooper   CS 8   UNIX Command Summary

ls	print the names of your files
cwho	find out who in our class is logged on
date	print the date
mail	read your mail (see below to send mail). Within **mail**:

    #   Print message number #
    d# Delete message number #
    q   Leave **mail**. Undeleted messages are put in file *mbox*
    ?   Ask mail for other command names
    Don't use the arrow keys to edit mistakes in mail.

rm *file*	remove file *file*
cp *old new*	make an extra copy of *old* named *new*
mv *old new*	change the name of file *old* to *new*
epr *file*	get a hard copy of *file* from the Evans basement 'user' lineprinter
cpr *file*	get a hard copy of *file* from the Evans basement 'counter' lineprinter
dpr *file*	get a hard copy of *file* from the 300 Davis lineprinter
more *file*	print *file* one screenful at a time
cat *file*	print *file* without stopping (<ctrl>S stops output)
man *command*	print the manual page for *comand*
vi *file*	prepare to edit *file* (**vi** commands on other side)
h	print a numbered list of the commands already given

The following commands are used to compile and run Pascal programs. Don't forget to recompile the program if you make any changes in it.

pi *prog.p*	compile a Pascal program
pie *prog.p*	as above, and print it (with errors) on the Evans basement 'user' printer
pic *prog.p*	as above, and print it (with errors) on the Evans basement 'counter' printer
pid *prog.p*	as above, and print it (with errors) on the 300 Davis lineprinter
px	run the compiled Pascal program

The following UNIX commands are ended by typing <ctrl>D

suggest
  suggestion...   Send an annonymous suggestion to the folks at the top
<ctrl>D

mail *recipient*
  letter...   Send a letter to *recipient*
<ctrl>D

At any time, <ctrl>S stops what's printing on the screen. Typing <return> starts printing again. The <break> key kills whatever is currently running (except **vi**).

<ctrl>U erase the current partial command—cancel the current line
<ctrl>H backspace (and erase)

TVI (standard) terminals only: Extra keys on the terminals are for use with another computer system. Your terminal will do weird things if you hit them, so DO NOT USE THE ARROW KEYS, FUNCTION KEYS, OR LOCAL EDITING KEYS. Stay away from the top row, period!

If <return> always moves the cursor to the left end of the current line, you've hit <shift> <block/conv> by accident. Fix the terminal with <ctrl> <block/conv>. Don't even wonder why.

Doug Cooper   CS 8   Second Week Assignment

Purpose

It's time to learn to use the editor, and to start writing programs. This assignment will either *a*) help you understand input, output, and assignment statements, give you practice in writing short programs, and show how Vi can help you write programs; or, *b*) kill you.

Try to give yourself a break by following these tips:

- Use all the different editing commands at least once.

- Get started early, and plan to get it graded early.

- Draft the programs on paper.

Due Dates

If the last letter of your account name is **a** through **m**, (e.g. c8-1ck) your homework is due Thursday through Sunday. If the last letter on your account is **n** through **z** (e.g. c8-1br) homework must be checked Saturday through Tuesday. Readers in the terminal room will check off your completed assignments.

Using The Editor

1.   Learning to use Vi is your most important job this week. I've given you a file named hunter (after Hunter Thompson, of course), whose contents are a mixed-up, misspelled version of the file named fran (that you sent to the lineprinter last week). Edit file hunter so that it approximates file fran.

I'm not concerned that you make a letter-for-letter duplicate. The point of this exercise is to give you practice using different Vi commands—not to test your typing or spelling. Don't just retype the entire file, even if that seems easiest. Try to use all the commands we discussed in class. The reader will test you by asking you to do some editing tasks.

Problems

2.   Write a program that prompts a user to enter a digit she particularly dislikes. Have the program multiply the number by 9, then multiply this product by 12345679 (notice the missing 8). Print out the final product.

3.   The Rabbitski sequence of numbers is formed by following this rule: Each number is the product of the two previous numbers. For example, the pair 2, 3 forms the Rabbitski sequence 6, 18, 108. Write a program that prompts for and reads in two numbers, then prints the first three numbers of the Rabbitski sequence they produce.

Try running both these programs with different inputs. The reader will look at your programs, and run them as well.

Special Note

The terminal room for our class is B40 Evans. Please do *not* log on from other terminal rooms. If no terminals are available in B40 Evans, start a waiting list for terminals on the blackboard. If somebody from another class is using terminals in B40 Evans, ask the TA or reader to ask them (nicely) to leave.

Technical explanation: There are only 28 terminal lines into the computer. If too many people try to log in, the terminal-connection device (the thing that says 'Request:') is supposed to keep track of who's waiting. Unfortunately, this device is really screwed up; when it says 'Connecting' or '2 Waiting' it is often lying. Even when it works, it's easy to miss your chance to log in (60 seconds) and go back to the end of the line again. So we keep the list on the blackboard instead. I have been requesting additional terminal lines for the past year and a half. We are all at the mercy of the Computer Center.

Doug Cooper   CS 8   Third Week Assignment

Purpose

Last week's assignment was fun, but now let's write some code that will give us answers we didn't know before we started! This assignment will require the use of functions and procedures, and will also show how the editor can help in program development.

As before, some good programming practice will save you a lot of grief in the long run:

- Get started early. Plan to get graded early—the terminal room will be jammed on Sunday and Tuesday.

- Draft the first program on paper, and have a friend 'run it' mentally for you.

- If you know your basic algorithm, work on parts of the program that you understand now, and leave harder sections as procedures to write later.

- If you're not sure about a Pascal detail, write a four or five line test program.

- Be sure to comment your code as you go along. This helps you understand what you're doing, as well as making the reader's job a lot easier.

Problems

1. Credit card companies often add a *check digit* to each card-user's account name. This value depends on the rest of the account name, and helps verify that the credit card is valid.

    Write a program that prompts for a credit card account name, then uses the algorithm given below to compute and print a check digit. Your program's input will be an account name that consists of a capital letter followed by 8 digits (e.g. A12345678). The name is entered all at once, and there are no spaces in the account name. The algorithm your program carries out is:

    - First, find the number represented by the letter, where 'A' represents 1, 'B' represents 2, and so forth.

    - Second, add that number to the sum of the four pairs of digits in the account name.

    - Third, find the *integer* remainder of dividing this number by 7. This is the check number.

    For example, suppose that 'E11223344' is a card number. Step 1 gives us 5, since 'E' is the fifth letter. In step 2, we add 5 to 11, 22, 33, and 44, yielding 115. In step 3, we find the *integer* remainder of a division by 7, which is 3. This is the check digit.

    HINT: Read in the digits as characters, rather than as numbers. Use the assignment statement shown on page 52 of *Oh! Pascal!* to find out the number each digit-character represents.

2. Create a program that has three procedures—the solutions to the problem given above, and the DislikedDigit and Rabbitski programs from last week. The statement part of the new program should consist of calls to the three procedures. It will be similar to the program on page 72 of the text.

    HINT: Make a file that contains the new program's heading and statement part. Then, use the vi command:

    :r *file* <esc>

    to read in each of the previously written programs. They won't need much modification to be turned into procedures.

Doug Cooper   CS 8   Fourth Week Assignment

Purpose

Last week's programs made no choices—they ran the exact same way, and executed the exact same statements, every single time. This week we'll use the **case** and **for** statements to make our programs a little less predictable.

This week's programs should give you practice with the **case** and **for** statements, and with value-parameters and variable-parameters. For more drill on the statements, do the Self-Test Exercises on pages 117-119. You should also study and learn to feel comfortable with parameters, since we'll use them in almost every assignment from now on.

- Write a few short test programs to clear up any problems you have with parameters. You must use parameters.

- It's better to have a working program that's not quite complete than it is to have a complete program that doesn't quite work. Learn to work around sticking points—don't let them stop you.

- Be sure to test your programs. Figure out what answer a certain set of input data should produce, and see if it works. Don't forget special cases like F− and A+.

Read the entire assignment before you start working. Having the final goal in mind will help you design your program most effectively.

Problem

Grade points are awarded at Berkeley on the following basis: A=4.0, B=3.0, C=2.0, D=1.0, and F=0.0 points. Letter grades can also be modified with a + (plus 0.3 point) or − (minus 0.3 points). Grade B+ counts as 3.3 points, while a C− is only 1.7 points.

Write a program that computes a grade-point average based on as many letter grades as the program user wants to enter. Your program should:

a)   explain what's going to happen, and ask the user how many grades will be entered;

b)   compute the number of grade points corresponding to each letter grade entered (one per line), and keep a running total of grade points;

c)   print the user's grade point average—the total divided by the number of grades entered.

Assume that every letter grade is followed by a '+', a '−', or a space. Be sure to deal with the special cases 'A+' (worth only 4.0 points), and 'F−' (worth only 0.0 points).

You can give the command **GPA** to run my version of this assignment, so you'll have an idea of what you're supposed to do. My program was about 60 lines long.

Hints

If you're not sure of how to proceed, write your program in stages. First, write a program that reads a letter grade, and prints out the corresponding numerical value. You'll find that using a variable to store the grade point value (rather than printing it out right away) will come in handy later. You can try my version of this program (it's about 35 lines long) by typing **Points**.

Second, rewrite this simple solution as a procedure. Assume that each letter and sign will be read by the main program *before* the procedure is called, and that the grade points will be output by the main program *after* the procedure call. Thus, the procedure needs three parameters—the letter, the sign, and the point-value variable. (Are they all value-parameters, all variable-parameters, or some of each?) No global variables should appear within the procedure, nor should the procedure print anything.

Bug Warning: Don't forget to get rid of the carriage return at the end of each input line.

(OPTIONAL—go-getters only!) The problem assumes that all grades carry the same weight. Write the program so that it gets and correctly uses the number of units for each class.

Doug Cooper   CS 8   Sixth Week Assignment

Purpose

How do you get to Carnegie Hall? Practice, practice, practice. This assignment provides practice in writing **if** statements, devising *boolean* expressions, using **repeat** and/or **while** statements, and declaring and passing parameters. The problems are both fairly short and sweet, so approach them as you might approach test problems—first pseudocode, then refine the pseudocode, and finally translate it into Pascal.

Be sure to draft your programs on paper first. 'Walk through' each program with a friend before you type it in. You'll find that pseudocode helps a lot when you start to write out *boolean* conditions.

Wherever possible, declare and pass parameters. They're one of the toughest features of Pascal—they're easy to understand when we go through an example in class, but they suddenly get complicated when it's time to use parameters in a program.

These problems count for 5% of your grade.

Problems

1. Write a program that asks the user how many numbers she wants to enter, then:

- Error-checks input by making sure that at least 1 and no more than 20 numbers are to be supplied;

- Determines and prints the average of the values entered;

- Finds and prints the largest and smallest values entered;

- Prints the positions of the largest and smallest values (counting from the first entry).

2. The January, 1984, issue of Scientific American contains an article (pp. 10−16) on an interesting sequence of numbers called a *hailstone series*. The article begins: 'Three steps forward and two steps back; it is not the most efficient way to travel, but it seems certain to get you there in the end.'

A hailstone series is formed in the following way: Take any number. If it is odd, triple the number and add one. If the number is even, divide by two. Continue until the series degenerates to the sequence 4, 2, 1, 4, 2, 1... You can imagine why this sequence is compared to a hailstone—every number goes up and down, getting larger and smaller, but eventually it falls to the 'ground' of 4, 2, 1. *

Write a program that asks the user for a positive starting integer no greater than 50,000, then finds two facts about the hailstone sequence it generates:

- How many steps does it take the sequence to reach one of the values 1, 2 or 4?

- What is the largest number the sequence reaches along the way?

You can use either a **while** or **repeat** loop. However, in either case, be sure to put in a maximum 'step' count of 500 (to guard against infinite loops).

If you are a go-getter, try to find out a few more facts about hailstone sequences by checking numbers automatically. What sequences starting under 100 have the greatest maximum value? What is the longest sequence starting with a number less than 100? How can you optimize your program to check higher numbers? **Please**: if you explore, do it when the system isn't crowded.

---

* This has been shown for all numbers up to 2^{40}, or about 1.2E12.

Doug Cooper   CS 8   First Project

Due: Part 1: 7th Week.   Part 2: 8th Week.   Part 3: 9th Week.

Purpose

During much of the rest of the term we'll be concerned with text processing—reading, printing, and acting upon character input. Text processing programs typically don't require complicated algorithms or code, but they almost always involve lots of detail. This assignment uses almost every control statement in Pascal (which is no problem because we know them all!). Time spent on this program is a good investment because *a)* you'll get practice writing many small code segments and procedures, and *b)* it shares some features of the final assignment.

- Pseudocode! Become intimately familiar with the job the program will do before you get involved with Pascal. A poor approach can make the program much harder than it really is. Go over your pseudocode with somebody before you code.

- Be modular. This program does many small jobs. It's better to have some of them working correctly than to have all of them not quite working. Get an idea of what parameters each program module will need.

- Look for similar commands. Divide the program commands into groups, rather than working on them at random. Leave the hardest ones for last.

- Don't type in the whole thing and hope for the best. Instead, stub program. Write a 'skeleton' main program that only knows about one or two commands, then add additional commands one at a time. If you're not sure about how to program individual commands, write them as simple programs first, or leave them as dummy procedures.

- Test the program as you write it. Test only one feature at a time. Use simple examples that test individual features before working on harder tests. You may never find a bug you don't test for.

- Document the program as you write it. Always assume that you are about to drop dead, and that your final grade in CS8 (which will follow you throughout Eternity) depends on your roommate being able to complete your program. Document any program shortcomings—this shows that you recognize the problem, and are in a good position to look for help.

- As in any real-life project, you will have to make judgements on how perfect a product you can produce. Use your time wisely—don't spend a lot of time on small or non-essential features. If you have to, pretend that a backup programmer is going to come in and upgrade your program, and leave comments for her to follow (e.g. 'Error check for valid command letter here').

Problem

A *text formatter* is a program that reads and echos characters, but is able to recognize and follow commands contained in the input text. Our problem is to write one. Assume that its input text will either be typed in, or supplied in a file. You can have your program get its input from a file named 'data' by typing:

        px < data

You should create your own test data files. It's a good idea to have test data that only checks one or two features at a time as you're working. The readers will have their own test files for checking your programs.

Your final program should recognize the commands listed on the reverse. Notice that each command begins with the character '#'.

This program is due in three parts. Parts 1 and 2 are graded Pass/No Pass, while Part 3—the entire program—receives a numerical grade that counts for 8% of your final grade. The reader may deduct up to 20% of your total for this assignment if you don't have parts 1 or 2 graded on time.

Part 1: Have your program recognize and follow these commands. You may assume that a numerical *count* is always supplied:

> #*count***S**   Print *count* blank lines. (Skip)
> #*count***R**   Print the next *count* letters, then carriage return. (Return)
> #*count***r**   Don't print the next *count* characters. (Rub-out)
> #*count***M**   Print the very next character *count* times. (Multiply)

You must write stub procedures for *all* command calls.

Part 2: Have your program recognize and follow these commands.

> #*count***C**   Capitalize the next *count* letters. (Capitalize)
> #*count***L**   Print the next *count* letters in lower-case. (Lower-case)
> #*count***I**   Indent the next line *count* spaces. (Indent)
> #*count***N**   Return, and number the next line with *count*. (Number)
> #*count***E**   Print the next *count* lines of input exactly as they appear. (Exact)
> #*count***P**   Make a new paragraph, indenting *count* spaces. (Pargraph)

Part 3: Have your program recognize and follow these commands. *In addition*, make the *count* value optional. If no *count* is supplied, make its default value is 1 (or 5 spaces for indenting commands).

> #*count***H**   Make the rest of the input line a capitalized, numbered, heading. (Heading)
> #*count***W**   Don't print the next *count* words. (Word)
> #*count***A**   Start making lines the shortest line longer than *count* letters.
>   Don't end the line in the middle of a word, though. (Adjust)

For all parts, all input text that isn't part of a command is just read and echoed. Your program need not worry about 'trick' input—while processing one command it won't ever read another command. (For instance, if the command is '#15C'—capitalize the next 15 letters—the next 15 letters won't include another command.) Nor will the input file end while a command is being carried out.

You will be able to run a sample version of the program by typing **format**. The command **format < data** will run the sample program on a test file named 'data.' By itself, the command **format** will let you use the sample program interactively. Type <ctrl>D on a line by itself to end the program.

I know that getting started is the hardest part, so here's a crucial segment from the main program:

```
    :
while not eof
  do begin
    read (Ch);
    if Ch = CommandMark
      then ObeyTheCommand
      else write (Ch)
  end
    :
```

Naturally, your program doesn't have to use this exact code. Good luck. A more detailed example of each command will be posted in the terminal room.

Doug Cooper   CS 8   Tenth Week Assignment

Purpose

This asssignment is intended to give you a little practice with defining and using arrays before you tackle the last major programming assignment. The first problem is adapted from an old final exam, and neither problem's solution is too long or too hard.

This assignment will be graded pass/fail. Concentrate on learning how to manipulate arrays—don't sweat over small details in the programs.

Problems

1. Write a program that reads a file of input text, finds the two letters that occur most frequently, then prints those letters, and the number of times each occurred. For example, given this input:

        bbbbcccddeaaaaa

    your program's output should say:

        a occurred 5 times
        b occurred 4 times

    A simple version of your program might assume that input consists of lower-case letters only.

    A general-purpose solution will count the frequency of both upper and lower-case letters.

    HINT: You will probably want to define:

    1) an array type whose index is the lower-case letters; or

    2) two arrays—one whose index is the upper-case letters, and one whose index is the lower-case letters.

2. Write a program that initializes a five-by-five array (to the values shown below), rotates that array 180 degrees, and then prints out the rotated array. The array should be initialized to these values:

            1 2 3 4 5
            6 7 8 9 10
           11 12 13 14 15
           16 17 18 19 20
           21 22 23 24 25

    The rotated array will be:

           25 24 23 22 21
           20 19 18 17 16
           15 14 13 12 11
           10 9 8 7 6
            5 4 3 2 1

    HINT: You may want to declare a second array (of the same type) to hold the rotated version of the original array; or, you might want to declare a procedure that lets you switch the elements in place, one pair at a time.

Doug Cooper   CS 8   Final Project

Due Dates: 1: 11th week   2: 12th week   13th week: HOLIDAY!   4: 14th week

Purpose

Our final assignment is to write an interactive text editor. To do well:

- Discuss different approaches to the problem. Come up with a plan of attack that takes advantage of the special skills of each group member. Make an informal contract of each member's responsibilities.

- Use stub programming techniques to make the program modular. Settle on parameters before you write subprogram code.

- Don't let one programmer take responsibility for anything bigger than a procedure.

- Look for underlying similarities between commands—are any commands just special cases of others? Are there any routines that more than one command might share?

- Bugs are an almost inescapable part of large programs. Build in code for debugging—procedures that print the values of variables, or the contents of your main data structure. Many hard-to-debug errors occur when you think your program contains certain data, while it actually holds wrong data, or no data at all.

- Make your program work, then make it robust. If you don't error-check, or don't implement all the program features, *document your decision*.

- Make the first version of your program a scale model. Only allow a 20-line text file, and 5-line maximum 'block' commands. **This is not a 'suggestion'— do it this way!**

Problem

Write a line-oriented text editor. Your editor will let a user modify the contents of an existing file, and permanently store the modified file. The final program should be able to handle files of up to 100 lines long, with up to 70 characters on each line. The maximum size of any 'block' move, copy, or append should be 50 lines. The commands are:

aN   Append new input after line N. Input ends when a period (.) appears on a line by itself, at the beginning of the line.

pM,N Print lines M through N. (You should number the lines to help you debug.)

P   Print the entire file being edited. (You should number lines during debugging.)

dM,N Delete lines M through N. Move remaining lines up to fill the hole.

mL,M,N Move lines M through N to after line L *instead of* their current place.

cL,M,N Copy lines M through N to after line L *as well as* their current place. (optional)

q   Leave the editor. Update the permanent stored file.

Q   Leave the editor without updating the permanent stored file.

? or h Help command. Print out a summary of editor commands.

For the following commands **M,N** means 'lines M through N.' M and N may be the same, but N must be greater than M.

fM,N/*word*/ Print each line, M through N, on which *word* appears.

sM,N/*old*//*new*/ Substitute *new* for each instance of *old* on lines M through N.

IM,N/*word*/

AM,N/*word*/

> Insert *word* at the beginning (or append *word* to the end) of lines M through N *only if it fits.*

We will discuss error-checking requirements in class.

Special Instructions

I'm supplying some extra non-standard code so that your text editor should be able to act on a file that already exists (and was possibly created using vi). You will be able to give the command: **px Text** to edit a file name Text. In effect, 'Text' is an argument to your program.

Although Standard Pascal, as discussed in the text, doesn't allow this sort of thing, Berkeley Pascal includes some extensions that let you take advantage of UNIX features. Since these extensions are rather confusing (besides being nonstandard), I've written two procedures that your program will use. The first, procedure GetTheFile, is used to read the argument file ('Text' in the example above) into the two-dimensional array that will be your program's main data structure.

The second procedure, RestoreTheFile, puts the contents of your two-dimensional array into the external file after it has been modified. If you don't want to save any of the changes you've made (by using the 'Q' command), you shouldn't call procedure RestoreTheFile. If RestoreTheFile *is* called, it should be the last action your program takes.

Commented versions of these two procedures can be found in your directory in a file named Extension. An uncommented version is in ShortExtension. Use the ':r *filename*' vi command to read either into your program file.

You may have to modify the heading of each procedure slightly by naming the type of your main data structure. Currently, it appears as 'var Work: Whole' in both procedures. The procedures should not be otherwise modified.

Due Dates

Like the formatter, this program will have weekly due dates. **Your final grade will lose up to 20% if you miss these deadlines.** However, they are pass/no pass. Their purpose is to make sure that you're making steady progress and to help iron out problems.

Your group due day (Sunday or Tuesday) is the due day of the majority of the group members.

For part 1, due at the end of the 11th week, you should have:

> Group Contract
> Driver, stub procedures for the entire
> program, and commands **p P q Q ? h**
> Each stub procedure should contain at least one *writeln*.

For part 2, due at the end of the 12th week, you should implement:

> **I A d** one of **m a**

For part 3, due at the end of the 13th week, you should take a break.

For final grading at the end of the 14th week, you should implement:

> **f s** the other of **m a**

Final grading will be scheduled in advance—each group will sign up for a half-hour meeting with two readers. **No work will be allowed after the first appointment.**

Grading

By and large, the programs will be graded as group efforts. In the absence of any objections, all group members will receive the same grade. However, group members can agree to distribute credit differently. A written contract between group members will help the readers understand each member's contribution.

The entire staff understands that not all groups will consist of equally dedicated programmers. Naturally, graders will take into account heroic efforts made by the remaining members of short-handed groups.

Suggestion

Begin this program in the same way as the formatter—with a driver, and stub procedures. As always, I appreciate that getting started is the hardest part, so here's a driver:

```
GetTheFile  {with the appropriate arguments}
repeat
   GetCommandLetter (Command);
   ObeyTheCommand (Command);
until Command in ['q', 'Q'];
```